We Have Honored the Children of Adam

Spiritual Guidance of the Naqshbandi Sufi Masters

By

Shaykh Nazim Adil Al-Haqqani

Foreword By

Shaykh Muhammad Hisham Kabbani

Institute for Spiritual and Cultural Advancement

© Copyright 2013 Institute for Spiritual and Cultural Advancement.

All rights reserved. No part of this book may be reproduced, stored in a retrieval system, or transmitted in any form, or by any means, electronic, mechanical, photocopying, or otherwise, without the written permission of the Institute for Spiritual and Cultural Advancement.

Library of Congress Cataloging-in-Publication Data

TBD

Published and Distributed by:

Institute for Spiritual and Cultural Advancement

17195 Silver Parkway, #401
Fenton, MI 48430 USA
Tel: (888) 278-6624
Fax:(810) 815-0518
Email: staff@naqshbandi.org

Web: http://www.naqshbandi.org

First Edition August 2013
ISBN: 978-1-938058-14-1

Author Mawlana Shaykh Muhammad Nazim Adil al-Haqqani, world leader of the Most Distinguished Naqshbandi-Haqqani Sufi Order.

Contents

About Shaykh Nazim vii
Foreword xv
Introduction xix
Publisher's Note xxiii
Notes xxiv
Preface xxv
Support for Our Souls Against Our Egos 1
Bring Sultans, Leave Tyranny 7
Concerning the Evils of this Time 15
Alive Hearts, Dead Hearts 23
The Importance of Learning Good Servanthood 32
Keeping Respect for All of Allah's Servants 41
Heavenly Patronage, Satanic Patronage" 49
The Fallacy of "Economic Crisis" Causing the People Misery ... 57
In Yesterday, Out Tomorrow 63
The High Honor of Addressing Our Lord by His Holy Name "Allah" . 70
The Power of Working for Allah 76
Concerning Slavery to Satan and Ego 84
Guarding Our Most Valuable Treasure 91
The Main Characteristic of Egos is Pride 98
Training Our Anger 104
Concerning Spirituality and Materiality 110
"Nothing Can Go Out of Its Private Line to Its Destiny" 117
"Contentment Is a Treasure that Is not Exhausted" 123
Avoiding Heavenly Anger Through Good Servanthood 129
Concerning "Modernized Islam" 138
The Source of Pleasure and Peace is Contentment 146
"Don't Ponder Over Allah but Ponder Over His Creation" . 152
The Greatness of the Grant of Our Creation 160

The Endless Honor Allah Gave to the Children of Adam	167
Glossary	175

About Shaykh Nazim

I had been fortunate enough to accompany the Shaykh together with his son-in-law, Shaykh Hisham Kabbani, in the United States in 1998 for a period of three weeks. During this time we toured New York, visited the United Nations and met with politicians on Capitol Hill in Washington.

Also part of the entourage were the muftis of Albania and Kosovo as well as the [late] Chechen president, Aslan Maskhadov. These activities were the precursor to the 2nd International Conference of the Islamic Supreme Council of America in Washington.

As the resident photographer I was privileged to witness first-hand something of the essence of the fortieth Grand Shaykh of the Naqshbandi Sufi order, an order that traces its lineage back in a "golden chain" to the Prophet Muhammad ﷺ through his greatest companion Abu Bakr as-Siddiq ؓ.

In 1998 I wrote that Shaykh Nazim was a spiritual colossus of the twentieth century. And while his contribution to the inner peace of humanity will never win him a Nobel Prize, it has to be remembered that at least half a million people have embraced Islam at his feet.

His *murids* (or followers) are said to run into millions and include heads of state, pop stars, and even allegedly Prince Charles. In that regard, I once heard Shaykh Nazim say that he was a collector of souls.

Of this I have no doubt, as in America I saw non-Muslims become mesmerised by his spiritual luminosity. In one instance I remember a crack junkie becoming a Muslim after meeting the Shaykh for two hours and in another, a CNN journalist saying *shahada* (Islam's testification of faith) after hearing him speak.

I saw complete strangers take his hand in the foyer of the United Nations, in the streets of New York and in the tree-lined avenues of Capitol Hill.

But in spite of all this, Shaykh Nazim remained down-to-earth, humble, sweet natured and loving to all. A pauper was treated as equally as a prince was in his company, and I never saw him ever turn anyone away.

His recent visit to Cape Town, South Africa, typified all of this. Whether playfully beating video man Dawood Schroeder with his stick on Table Mountain, bantering with tourists, or conversing with the late Shaykh Nazim Mohamed at the Muslim Judicial Council, he was always at the same time serious, witty and incredibly insightful.

His apparently simple *sohbets* or talks were often exactly the opposite, deep, cryptic, metaphysical - and extremely challenging. I mean, for example, how many 'alims can explain ibn 'Arabi's *wahdat al-wujud* (the unity of being) in three sentences?

After witnessing him in action for a week in Cape Town, my feelings about Shaykh Nazim have been reconfirmed. Yes, he is definitely a spiritual giant of our times. But in so saying, describing him has become even more difficult! ...

As a multi-layered personality, Shaykh Nazim is many things to many people. In his presence, one feels strangely secure. He is definitely the kind of person you would like to share a bomb shelter with.

As a person who treads lightly in the *dunya* he may appear soft and bending (like the proverb of the Malaysian rice plant in the wind) but when it comes to submitting to his Creator, he is unwavering. Here, it is easy to sense that his iman is like steel.

Perhaps the uniqueness of Shaykh Nazim in this arrogant day and age is his manner of approach. His presence does not announce itself to you as king or conqueror but rather as a servant. What is so engaging is that he essentially humbles himself to you with a fine-tuned subtlety before you realise that you must humble yourself to him.

One of his favourite English expressions is "Mercy Oceans," his Grand Shaykh 'Abdullah ad-Daghestani's way of explaining the Sunnah and its countless mercies. And for those who think the Sunnah—the way of our beloved master Muhammad ﷺ —is a simple matter of beard length and counting the rewards like bank notes, there is a very rude awakening.

For Shaykh Nazim the Sunnah is strict Shari'ah—as well as charity, generosity, hard work, heart knowledge and compassion.

Of all the people I have encountered on this earth, Sayyid Mawlana Shaykh Nazim Adil al-Haqqani is the closest I have seen anybody come to epitomise the Sunnah. In his commanding presence I felt like an unclean grain of sand being washed around in the depths of his "Mercy Oceans."

I remember him once saying on the lawn of a *murid*'s house: "My people, are you happy? Allah is happy. The Angels are happy. They are not for crying..." Indeed, in just a few words he had taught us the excellence of a positive outlook on life and the fact that other people's hearts will open like flowers to a smile.

But on a deeper level with these simple words he had actually taught the real lesson, the *adab* of viceregency.

In another instance he said that man was chasing zeroes. "Are you going to show your checkbook to Allah?" he asked with a chuckle. "The aim of mankind today is to collect zeroes, but you have been created for Allah's divine service. Service for *dunya* is not for Allah Almighty..."

After being rudely challenged from the floor in a Cape Town mosque and accused of contravening the Sunnah, Shaykh Nazim came up with the following *sohbet* a few hours later.

"Rasulullah [1] called people to him, he was a saviour of souls. Some came to him saying 'save our souls' and he saved them as they surrendered. These (pious) people were respected whether living or dead. Shaytan became angry because of this...

"Shaytan becomes angry if a saved person is (particularly) from the sahabis or the *awliya*. Shaytan wants these people to be taken away. He is the biggest enemy of the pious. People destroy tombs and *mazars* of the *awliya* because

---

[1] stands for "*Salla-Lahu 'alayhi wa sallam,*" meaning, "Allah's peace and blessings be upon him," the Islamic invocation for Prophet Muhammad.

Shaytan asks for them not to be known. He wants the ummah to forget them...that's the reason for no tombstones!

"Allah says don't forget people who did their best for Me, these people who gave their souls for Islam, but Shaytan wants them to be forgotten. Shaytan wants his people to destroy everything that was against Shaytan. Shaytan is crying for his hatred..Shaytan (is jealous of good) and wants to destroy the graves of those who killed Abu Jahl..."

It was a devastating critique of the Salafis but no less a serious warning directed at our very own *nafs*.

I could go on forever quoting Shaykh Nazim's pearls of wisdom dropped into the "Mercy Oceans" net for the seeker throughout the day. In nearly a month of observing his behaviour I have never seen him talk from notes. He sleeps little and his day starts well before Fajr (dawn) and often ends in the early hours of the morning.

For those who challenge the credentials of Shaykh Nazim it is perhaps best to remember that he is an orthodox Sunni Muslim down to his fingertips and studied Shari'ah, Qur'anic sciences and Hadith under great masters in Turkey, Syria and the Lebanon.

He is the mufti of Turkish Cyprus and is an acknowledged *'alim* of Hanafi *fiqh*, apart from possessing a Masters Degree in Chemical Engineering from Istanbul University.

Academic qualifications aside, Shaykh Nazim is a Sayyid (a descendent of the Holy Prophet ﷺ) on both the Hasani and Husayni lines. Through his father he traces his lineage back to Sayyid 'Abdul Qadir Jilani ؓ (the great 10th century saint) and through his mother to Mawlana Jalaluddin Rumi ؓ.

As a Grand-Shaykh of the Naqshbandi tariqat Shaykh Nazim also carries *ijazah* (permission to teach) in other orders such as the Qadiri and Rifa'i'.

Physically, Shaykh Nazim is small of stature but somehow seems to be much taller than he actually is. He may well be past his 80th year, but when he strides out (his walking stick before him like an *alif*), it's always as if one is trying to keep up with him. I have also never seen him miss his *salat*, even when on travel... He has performed the Hajj 27 times, has undergone rigorous spiritual seclusion on many occasions and has established Islamic centres around the world.

Indeed, the *baraka* of Shaykh Nazim spreads wherever he travels. Cape Town was no exception. A person I know was embraced by the Shaykh and shortly afterwards dreamt of Sayyidina Abu Bakr ﷺ. Another who had not met Shaykh Nazim or any of his entourage was given advice in a dream by one of his *khalifas* (Shaykh Hisham).

A moment on his last night in a country mosque outside Cape Town will stay in the memory for a long time. Shaykh Nazim had asked the question: "What goodness has the modern (university) graduate brought to society without the Holy Books?" After suggesting that "Tariqat says keep Sunnah, the essence of Shari'ah," he then went on to talk about the threat of secularism.

"Oh my people, 20th century education is aimed at bringing people to the level of animals...higher education is not leading to Allah when the name of Allah is prohibited," he said.

"We are living in a time that truth is lost and defenders of truth have disappeared…I ask for you to be defenders of truth."

The "Oh my people" rang like a bell. "Oh my ummah!" At that moment it seemed as if it was not Shaykh Nazim talking, but the Prophet ﷺ. Shaykh Nazim had become the Sunnah! Great men, friends of Allah, who see with the eyes of Allah and whose hearts beat with the unison of the *kalimah*, enjoy vision through the agency of the Prophet ﷺ.

Perhaps, in conclusion, it would be fitting to recall something remarkably profound that Shaykh Nazim uttered on top of Table Mountain, an event that lent itself to much symbolism. Before that the Shaykh had "communed" with nature, admiring the view of the city and ocean 1,000 metres below and playfully eying a rock rabbit.

As Hafiz Mahmoud Sahib made the *adhan* for Dhuhr, a bird on a ledge before him sang its heart out. After making Dhuhr *salat* on one of the viewing platforms that faced north from the southernmost city of Africa, he turned around and then challenged those in Cape Town who had been attacking him but who had declined to confront him in debate.

"They come here, we all jump together, and then we see who floats," he said, ominously waving his hand like a butterfly settling on a flower.

Shafiq Morton
Cape Town, South Africa
November, 2000

Copyright al-Qalam Magazine

Foreword

Bismillahi-r-Rahmani-r-Raheem
In the Name of God, the Most Beneficent, the Most Merciful

All praise is due to God Almighty, Allah the Exalted and Bounteous and the most fluent, abundant and sweet praise and blessings be upon His perfect servant, the mercy to all creation and exemplar of perfect character, ethics and morality Prophet Muhammad ﷺ, and upon his family and Companions.

This book is a compendium of *sohbets* or spiritual discourses by our master—chief of saints and reviver of the Prophetic path to divine enlightenment, teacher of millions and worldwide leader of the Naqshbandi-Haqqani Sufi Order, Mawlana Shaykh Muhammad Nazim Adil al-Haqqani, may Allah grant him health and long life.

It is related that in the Last Days of this world—which, based upon the predicted indications is taking place even as I pen these words—those who adhere to the pure teachings of the prophets and saints will become rare. On the contrary, those who breach the Prophetic Tradition, the Sunnah, will be commonplace.

No prior prophet ever mentioned in such detail what Prophet Muhammad ﷺ foretold fourteen hundred years ago. In the seventh century, he gave a precise description with specific details which were not fully understood until their manifestation in the present age. The Prophet ﷺ explained what would transpire in the Last Days so that the people witnessing those events could recognize their place in time. The Prophet ﷺ warned that when bedouin Arabs compete to construct lofty buildings in the desert the Hour of Judgment would be close. He predicted that in the Last Days, trustworthy people would be vilified regarded as traitors by the people.

In a Prophetic Tradition[2] it is related that a bedouin came to Prophet Muhammad ﷺ and asked when Judgment Day would take place. He said, "When the trust (*al-amana*) is lost, then await Judgment Day." The bedouin asked, "How will it be lost?" The Prophet ﷺ replied, "When power and authority comes in the hands of unfit persons, then wait for the Judgment Day."[3] He also has said that "the trustworthy one will be called a traitor."

As the Prophet ﷺ predicted, the psychology of people in our time is the opposite of what is prescribed and it is nearly impossible to find a trustworthy person. At the same time, everywhere on earth, different groups are busy destroying what remains of faith and spirituality, each one following its own agenda. Even "spiritual" groups and individuals slander each other, and through their corrupt behavior, support falsehood—all the while claiming to be believers.

The words of the tradition, "The trustworthy, *al-amin*, one will be said to be a traitor," has an interpretation. Al-Amin is one of the names of Prophet Muhammad ﷺ, and one of the signs of the Last Days is that people will attack the Prophets of God, in particular the Last Messenger,

---

[2] Arabic: *hadith*.
[3] Sahih Bukhari.

Muhammad ﷺ, and the message he brought for mankind's felicity.

Alhamdulillah—praise God—we are fortunate to be students or disciples of Mawlana Shaykh Nazim. As long as he, and Sufi masters like him, continue to teach the ways of the the prophets and saints, hope remains for humankind. For his teachings, while outwardly plain, are endowed with a wisdom and grace seldom found today. The shaykh's words take you back to a simpler time, when people were straightforward, when they what they meant, and when they did what they said.

May God bless you as you pick up this volume and read some of the holy teachings he has brought. It is well known in the Naqshbandi Sufi tradition, that pure words of guidance are able to elevate the reader to the stations and states described simply through the blessed character, *baraka,* of one authorized to teach them. Futher, these teachings will remain with you and part of you in this life and on, into the hereafter.

I am only a student and I have been learning from my teacher Mawlana Shaykh Nazim, who, despite his 85 years of age is still incredibly active spreading the teachings that come to his heart from the spiritual "central headquarters." What I saw and learned from my master I cannot express because those fountains are always pouring forth, continuously flowing. The hearts of such saints are like waterfalls: giving always and they are not asking to take anything, asking only to give.

As the world around us seems to slide further into its darkest chapter, in a time when negativity and skepticism insistently challenge faith, the faithful of all beliefs seek a beacon that will lead them to a divine shelter of peace and protection. Presented in this volume are essential aspects of a spiritual discipline which dates back to the time when Prophet Muhammad delivered the divine message—a message preserved by Sufi masters over forty generations.

In these times when Islam is more and more visible on the world stage, it is hoped through this humble work that readers will come to better understand the true teachings of Islam, namely, the universal endorsement to practice moderation and follow the middle course, to hold patience, to uphold tolerance and respect for others, to approach conflict resolution in peaceful ways, to condemn all forms of terrorism, and above all, to love God, appreciate His Divine favors, and strive in His divine service. The greatest Islamic teaching is that there is no higher station than to serve the Lord Almighty.

Shaykh Muhammad Hisham Kabbani
Fenton, Michigan
October 28, 2007

INTRODUCTION

Endless praise and thanks be to God Most High, who guides His servants to His light by means of other servants of His whose hearts He illuminates with His divine love.

Since the beginning of human history, God Most High has conveyed His revealed guidance to mankind through His prophets and messengers, beginning with the first man, Adam ﷺ. The prophetic line includes such well-known names as Noah, Abraham, Ishmael, Isaac, Jacob, Joseph, Lot, Moses, David, Solomon, and Jesus, peace be upon them all, ending and culminating in Muhammad, the Seal of the Prophets ﷺ, a descendant of Abraham ﷺ, ﷺwho brought the final revelation from God to all mankind.

But although there are no longer prophets upon the earth, the Most Merciful Lord has not left His servants without inspired teachers and guides. *Awliya*—holy people or saints—are the inheritors of the prophets. Up to the Last Day, these "friends of God," the radiant beacons of truth, righteousness and the highest spirituality, will continue in the footsteps of the prophets, calling people to their Lord and guiding seekers to His glorious Divine Presence.

One such inspired teacher, a shaykh or *murshid* of the Naqshbandi Sufi Order, is Shaykh Nazim Adil al-Qubrusi al-Haqqani. A descendant not only of the Holy Prophet Muhammad ﷺ but also of the great Sufi masters 'Abul Qadir Gilani and Jalaluddin Rumi, Shaykh Nazim was born in Larnaca, Cyprus, in 1922 during the period of British rule of the island. Gifted from earliest childhood with an extraordinarily spiritual personality, Shaykh Nazim received his spiritual training in Damascus at the hands of Mawlana Shaykh 'Abdullah ad-Daghestani (fondly referred to as "Grandshaykh"), the mentor of such well-known figures as Gurjieff and J. G. Bennett, over a period of forty years.

Before leaving this life in 1973, Grandshaykh designated Shaykh Nazim as his successor. In 1974, Shaykh Nazim went to London for the first time, thus initiating what was to become a yearly practice during the month of Ramadan up to 1990s. A small circle of followers began to grow around him, eagerly taking their training in the ways of Islam and *tariqah* at his hands.

From this humble beginning, the circle has grown to include thousands of *murids* or disciples in various countries of the world, among whom are to be found many eminent individuals, both religious and secular. Shaykh Nazim is a luminous, tremendously impressive spiritual personality, radiating love, compassion and goodness. He is regarded by many of his *murids* as the *qutub* or chief saint of this time.

The shaykh teaches through a subtle interweaving of personal example and talks ("Associations" or *sohbets*), invariably delivered extempore according to the inspirations that are given to him. He does not lecture, but rather pours out from his heart into the hearts of his listeners such knowledge and wisdoms as may change their innermost beings and bring them toward their Lord as His humble, willing, loving servants.

Shaykh Nazim's language and style are unique, so eloquent, moving and flavorful that not only do his teachings seem inspired but also his extraordinary use of words. His *sohbets* represent the teachings of a twentieth century Sufi master, firmly grounded in Islamic orthodoxy, speaking to the hearts of the seekers of God of any faith tradition from his own great, wide heart, in a tremendous outpouring of truth, wisdom and divine knowledge which is surely unparalleled in the English language, guiding the seeker toward the Divine Presence.

The sum total of Shaykh Nazim's message is that of hope, love, mercy and reassurance. In a troubled and uncertain world in which old, time-honored values have given place to new ones of confused origins and unclear prospects, in which a feeling heart and thinking mind is constantly troubled by a sense of things being terribly disordered and out of control, in which the future seems forebodingly dark and uncertain for humanity, he proclaims God's love and care for His servants, and invites them to give their hearts to Him.

Shaykh Nazim holds out to seekers the assurance that even their smallest steps toward their Lord will not go unnoticed and unresponded to. Rather than threatening sinners with the prospect of eternal Hell, he offers hope of salvation from the Most Merciful Lord, and heart-warming encouragement and incentive for inner change and growth. As one who has traversed every step of the seeker's path and reached its pinnacle, he offers both inner and practical guidelines for attaining the highest spiritual goals.

The talks in this book were given in spring 2004, at Mawlana's home in Cyprus. Each of these talks is entirely extempore, as Shaykh Nazim never prepares his words but invariably speaks according to inspirations coming to his heart.

In keeping with the shaykh's methodology—the methodology of the prophets, particularly of the Last Prophet, Muhammad, peace be upon him and upon them all, and of the Qur'an itself—of reinforcing vital lessons by repetition and reiteration, the same themes and anecdotes recur again and again. The talks seem to come in unannounced clusters, centering around a primary theme, which develops and evolves according to the spiritual state of the listeners. Thus, Shaykh Nazim may cite the same verse or *hadith*, or tell the same tale on different occasions, each time reinforcing a slightly different aspect of the eternal message of love and light which is Islam.

The shaykh's talks are interspersed with words and phrases from Arabic and other Islamic languages. These are translated either in the text itself, in footnotes the first time they occur, or, for general and recurrent terms, in the Glossary at the end of this volume. Qur'anic verses quoted in the text have been referenced for easy access.

Every attempt has been made to retain the shaykh's original language with minimal editing. However, since these talks were transcribed from audio tapes recorded on amateur equipment by listeners for their own personal use (or, in the case this volume, by a *murid* extremely familiar with the shaykh's language and ideas, by hand), some inadvertent errors may have found their way into the text. For these, we ask Allah's forgiveness and your kind indulgence. May He fill your heart with light and love as you read and reflect upon these inspired words, and guide you safely to His exalted Divine Presence.

Publisher's Note

Shaykh Nazim is fluent in Arabic, Turkish and Greek, and semi-fluent in Engish. Over three decades, his llectures have been transated into twenty or more languages, and to date have reached the furthest corners of the globe. We sincerely hope the reader will appreciate the author's unique language style, which has been painstakingly preserved in this work.

As some of the terms in this book may be foreign, to assist the reader we have provded transliterations, as well as a detailed glossary.

NOTES

The following symbols are universally recognized and have been respectfully included in this work:

The symbol ﷺ represents *sall-Allahu 'alayhi wa sallam* (Allah's blessings and greetings of peace be upon him), which is customarily recited after reading or pronouncing the holy name of Prophet Muhammad ﷺ.

The symbol ؏ represents *'alayhi 's-salam* (peace be upon him/her), which is customarily recited after reading or pronouncing the holy names of the other prophets, family members of Prophet Muhammad ﷺ, the pure and virtuous women in Islam, and the angels.

The symbol ؓ/ؓ represents *radi-Allahu 'anhu/'anha* (may Allah be pleased with him/her), which is customarily recited after reading or pronouncing the holy names of Companions of the Prophet ﷺ.

PREFACE

In the Name of Allah, The Beneficent and The Munificent

This, my English, is strange English. Not everyone can understand because, *subhanallah*, meanings are coming to my heart, and when running in my heart to give to you, I am using any means – from here, from there - bringing any word which may be useful.

I am like a person waiting for water to run out from the faucet. Then, when suddenly it comes, and he knows the water is going to be turned off, stop running, he may take any container – with a no-good shape, broken on one side, or anything he may find there – quickly bringing them to take that water and store it. Therefore, when meanings are coming to my heart, I am trying to explain with any word, which you may understand or not. But you must understand, because we have a saying, "Listeners must be more wise than speakers." Therefore, when inspiration comes, we must explain.

They are living words, not plastic – bananas, plastic; apples, plastic, and grapes. Even if the shapes are not much, they are living, real. When you are going to arrange them in measures, good system; when you are going to be engaged by outside forms, you are losing meanings. ▲

1

SUPPORT FOR OUR SOULS AGAINST OUR EGOS

A'udhu bil-Lahi min ash-Shaytani-r-rajeem. Bismillahi-r-Rahmani-r-Raheem. La hawla wa la quwwata illa bil-Lahi-l-'Aliyi-l-'Azheem.

It is an Association, maybe a short meeting, a little bit more than a quarter of an hour, or half-an-hour or one hour. According to our deep desire, what we may be in need of, They are giving.[1]

A small motorcycle may come to a petrol station and say, "Fill it." Its capacity is only one liter, taking it away. Sometimes there comes a forty-wheel lorry, from here up to my home. Forty wheels is going to take two barrels of petrol. According to their work, they may take.

Now we are here. What you are in need of, They may give; and we are only a mediator. That means a pipe coming from Them and giving. We are in need. As each day our physical being needs eating and drinking, our spirituali-

---

[1] The departed grandshaykhs of the Naqshbandi *Tariqah*, from whom inspirations come to Shaykh Nazim's heart.

ty is also in need of power. It is powerful enough, but it is in most need to take away our ego's pressure.

Our egos are making a wall around our spirituality, never letting it show its mission and its power. Always coming, our egos, and saying, "I am here, I am here. First *I* must be satisfied, and then you may come and do as you like." And our ego is never going to finish. Up to the last moment when we leave this life, it wants to continue its control, its power over us, wanting not to give any chance to our spirituality, saying, "I am first here. When I am finished, you may come and act." And till we pass away, our physical desires or needs are never-ending.

And we are trying to advise, as all prophets advised mankind. It is only to give support to our souls, to defeat our ego's pressure on our souls. Commonly, people are under the pressure of their egos, and as long as people under their egos' pressure, no way for souls to do anything or to show their power.

As an example, we may say that a person is in prison and surrounded by guards, never letting that person get out, and sometimes people try to make a way to save that one from prison. And all the prophets, and particularly the Seal of the Prophets ﷺ,[2] just came to make a way for our imprisoned souls to take their freedom, to be free. When your souls are going to be free, quickly you are going to be in relationship with Heavens—quickly, and you are free.

---

[2] This Arabic logo stands for "*Sallallahu 'alaihi wa sallam,* may Allah's peace and blessings be on him," the Islamic invocation for Prophet Muhammad ﷺ.

But people are understanding freedom in another way: freedom for our physical desires. They want freedom such that no hindrance should be put in front of them for reaching their physical desires and enjoyments. That is their freedom! And then they are first breaking religious restraints that do not give a chance to ego to be free; because when you give freedom to your ego, it quickly runs to Shaytan[3] and says, "I am with you. I am a volunteer. Whatever you say, I will do. I am free!"

Therefore, shaytanic groups, Shaytan's representatives, are first attacking beliefs so that no one should believe in anything. They are using so many wrong ways, and they want to teach and to make people believe that we are material beings, and that beyond materiality and materialism there is nothing. And they are putting that as a base for their teaching, for their lives, for their civilization, for everything.

They are building on materiality and materialism, and materialism makes people say, "No God," makes people not believe in anything beyond materiality. They are saying, "We must see a thing. If we do not see and touch a thing, we do not accept it—no, no!" And up to today they are doing this. They are not taking any care now.

That is their theory, their aim—to make people not say that there is anything beyond materiality, to make people free from beliefs, free from religions, and to make the value of prophets at the lowest level. And they are saying, "Those people never existed on earth. All of them are fictions. Don't believe!"

---

[3]Satan.

The main aim of all teaching in the twenty-first century is to teach youngsters not to believe. "If you want freedom, you must not believe in anything! Then you are free. Beliefs are the biggest hindrance for you to reach your aims, your physical desires—the biggest hindrance. Destroy them, and you should reach freedom."

It is one hundred per cent wrong because that kind of freedom is destroying generations physically, mentally, spiritually. The real freedom that prophets brought from Heavens is to make a person free from his or her physical desires. And the first step for that purpose is that you must use materiality only to stand on, not to be under its command, using materiality only for certain purposes, to support your physical being within its limits.[4] But when people go beyond the limits for their physical being's desires, they should be *asir*, captured, captured by devils. They want unlimited fulfillment for their physical desires, and it is impossible.

Therefore, every religion brings orders about things that should be done and some other orders about forbidden things that you must not approach. Otherwise, you are been caught, you are captured. Keep yourself on this side. On the other side is Shaytan, saying, "This side is absolute freedom for you." But it is *never* going to be freedom for you. It may destroy your physical being, and you may lose every chance for your spirituality.

And we are advising. It is a humble meeting, but what we are saying is important for all mankind, because realities

---

[4] To fulfill their legitimate physical needs.

can't be changed by the passing of centuries or by peoples' imagination, no. Reality is not imaginary; it is fixed. Reality is fixed, but imagination is never going to be fixed. Therefore, prophets were sent to teach people.

O people, ask for Reality for your lives. What is the reality of being a human being, what is the reality of your having been put on this planet? Ask for Reality regarding it; don't use *nadhariyah*, theories—no. All theories are imagination, not Reality.

Ask for Reality—why you are in existence, why you are on this planet. Unchanged Reality, you can find there. And prophets came to say this, to make people understand this point. If understanding, they are going to reach to Reality. Otherwise, they will be with their imaginings, and imagining never give anything to them. And they are going to be destroyed and disappear.

Shaytan, shaytanic teachings, are calling people to an imagined life. And youngsters, particularly, are always imagining something like freedom for every desire, and it is impossible. It is not Reality to reach a point at which you can be free and taste something with your physical being each time, and without its getting less but getting more. That is all imagination. Each day's advice, the biggest advice, is to call people to Reality. And shaytanic advice is to call people to imagination.

Heavenly teachings are calling people to Reality, but our ego is always coming first and wanting to impose its authority and power on your real being, your soul, because souls' being is Reality, and Reality is never going to be changed. But our physical being, it is only an appearance, an imagination, because it is going to be finished and vanish, nothing more.

After one hundred years, no one here should be in existence—finished! If our physical being were real being, it would not disappear, it would be continuous. But it is only an imaginary figure, to be used for a short life, for some wisdoms, for some reasons that people are informed about in heavenly books.[5] And our real being that gives our personality, that is our soul. Souls are real beings, never going to disappear. Their being, their existence, is continuous.

May Allah save us from being cheated by satanic teachings! But I am sorry to say that everywhere people are calling to shaytanic ways and making life a charming image for people, and people are running after it. And finally, they are going to look to find something. But they will never find anything, and they will say, "Oh-h, it was a mirage! We ran after it throughout our whole lives, and now we are here and we are finding nothing. It was a mirage."

Before repenting for such a mistake, try to accept Reality, what is real of your being. You should be happy here and Hereafter, and make your Lord, Almighty Allah, happy with you and pleased with you.

May Allah forgive us! For the honour of the most honoured one in His Divine Presence, Sayyidina Muhammad ﷺ—*Fateha!* ▲

---

[5]The sacred scriptures of the three monotheistic, revelation-based faiths, Islam, Judaism and Christianity.

2

BRING SULTANS, LEAVE TYRANNY

A'udhu bil-Lahi min ash-Shaytani-r-rajeem. Bismillahi-r-Rahmani-r-Raheem. La hawla wa la quwwata illa bil-Lahi-l-'Aliyi-l-'Azheem.

We are asking for protection from evil and from devils. And when a person asks for protection, that means that he is *y'atiraf*, admitting, that he is weak and helpless. Admitting is the sign of servanthood. A servant knows that he is weak and that his Owner is powerful.

Our Grandshaykh, Shaykh 'Abdullah ad-Dhagestani, *Sultan ul-Awliya*,[1] was always saying that the loveliest characteristic that Allah Almighty likes to see in His servant is admitting his weakness. A weak person says that I can't do anything because I am weak. Those people who claim, "I am powerful," are showing their power, and because of their power most of them have pride.

To be proud is the characteristic of Shaytan because Shaytan was claiming, "I am such-and-such a one. I am a

---

[1] Shaykh Nazim's predecessor and shaykh, who passed away in 1973. *Sultan ul-Awliya:* the Sultan of [Muslim] Saints.

more powerful, more honourable, more respected one.[2] That Adam, I do not accept him because in my sight he is not as honourable a one as I am. I was created before him, and for hundreds and thousands of years I have been giving my servanthood, my worship. That one is a new creature, not yet making even one *sajdah*,[3] but he has been granted that honour. Why? I am the honourable one, but he is not honourable!"

He was thinking that honour is granted according to a person's works or efforts. If it were according to our works that we are granted honour, a worker would be much more honoured than the *sultan*. The *sultan* does not work. The *sultan* sits on his throne, but his workers—in his palace, in his kitchens, in his gardens, and for this and that purpose—work hard, while the *sultan* only sits. If, we might say, the *sultan's* throne was empty and Shaytan was a worker, he would think that that throne should be for him. He would image or he would look at himself and say, "Oh! That throne is so suitable for me. Must be for me," because he would look around himself and say, "No one is like me for worshipping and knowing. Oh-h, that throne is so suitable for me, and the honour of that most honourable throne should be given to me!" Yes.

When a *sultan* passes away, someone from his line comes to that throne because his level is not the level of common people, and common people must have someone above their level. If you do not bring a king or *sultan* and

---

[2] Qur'an, 2:34, 7:12, 15:31-33, 17:61, 18:50, 20:11, 38:76.
[3] Prostration.

put him on that throne, people are going to fight each other to reach that honour. Everyone may say, "I am suitable for that." But their level is the common level. No one is going to be happy for someone from their level or from their line to be on that throne, saying, "Why? You are like me, also." But when a *sultan* passes away and the crown prince comes from his line, people say, "Yes, he is all right, this one. That honour is for him because he comes from the line of his father, from the king's line, not from the common line." But now you are seeing those satanic traps and tricks, making people believe that there is no need for the line of kings, the line of *sultans*. "That honour must be also for *you*. Therefore, take them away!"

It began from 1789, the great French Revolution, that opened the door for tyrants. And people are in a poisoned atmosphere that they are not finding a way to get out of, to breathe clean air and to learn servanthood, *mu'amalah*[4] — how to be a servant; because the way of being a servant, servanthood, can be learned when they keep their *sultan* and the *sultan's* honour and respect, and they learn that they must be respectful, also, to their Creator, to Allah Almighty.

Therefore, Shaytan is coming and taking away everything by which people can learn how they should be respectful servants to their Lord. They learned that when they had kings or *sultans*. Now, after they took that away, they are saying, "You and I are equal. You have a chance to be president, I have a chance to be president; you have a chance to be *sultan*, I have a chance to be *sultan*."

---

[4]Behavior, conduct, treatment, mutual relations.

Then, finished! *Fasad*, corruption, just began from that time. They killed their king and queen and their descendants, *asılzade*, nobility. They killed everyone, even little ones, under the guillotine, the French people who claim that they are the most civilized people, first class. They destroyed respect and they lost the respect of the common people for their kings or *sultans*. And after that, all nations learned from the French Revolution, and one after another they also fought their kings and *sultans*, taking them away, and then they came in power.

Now the whole world is full of unsolved problems, never-ending troubles and unbearable sufferings. People have fallen into it. Therefore, now this world can't have peace till they bring to power mediators, who are their kings and *sultans*, so that they may respect their Lord because they have learned how they should give respect.

Now, children, are not giving respect to their parents; students are not giving any respect to their teachers; common people are not giving any respect to their M.P.s or governments. They are fighting; each day now you see the streets full of disobedient servants. No respect! People are running like rivers in the streets and fighting governments and killing, and they are going to be killed. No respect; finished!

This is the time of tyrants. Tyrants, no mercy in their hearts; they may kill, they may do any kind of bad thing to common people. You see that they are hitting them, they are putting them in jails and giving so many punishments that the bodies of people can't bear. They may die but they never take any responsibility. They just say, "He died"—

from beating, from bad treatment of them. Every kind of punishment is giving trouble to those people in jails; they are finishing and no one is asking. Tyrants, no mercy in their hearts, no justice, no respect for people, nothing of good characteristics among tyrants. You must not ask!

Therefore, now people are running in the streets. They are asking for someone, someone like before, to be respected. But they are going to have at least two parties, one bringing their chief ones, their heads, for a short time, and after that, the other group grows and comes, taking them away. Then they get up and say, "Why? This is a bad one. We must have a new election!"

What election? If you do not bring your *sultan* or your king, in an election—this this party winning today, the other saying, "He is not doing good; we must bring our side, and this and that, this and that"—this fighting will continue.

Shaytan has been working on it from the beginning of history. That history, they are say, began in Egypt. Their heads had kingdoms. The king, pharaoh, was able to make people respect him. No one was able to stand up against him; if standing up, he was quickly taken away. Always power was with the rulers, up to the beginning of the nineteenth century. And Shaytan was working on it, especially on that point of taking away the heads of nations, their kings and *sultans*, to make people come and fight among themselves.

Now we are saying this about shaytanic teachings: Shaytan was expecting that that throne must be for me. And he was thinking of having democracy in the Divine

Presence, thinking of making an election, of asking the angels [chuckles], "Who is suitable for this throne?" And all the angels would say, "You are our teacher and you are such a person. We think that you are suitable for that throne."

He was thinking of having democracy in the Heavens [laughs]. But Allah Almighty was saying, ordering, "*I* am bringing a noble one among creation and *I* am dressing him from My honour. In divine honour I am dressing him, making him My deputy, and for that reason I am putting him on that throne, not you.

"I am dressing that honour on *him*, not on you. And that dress does not need too many things to work. No, no need. *I* am that One who puts an honourable dress on anyone I please—finished! I am not looking at their works, I am looking at who is suitable to be dressed in that dress of divine honour.

"Adam, you sit there, and you [Iblis] make *sajdah* to him. Prostrate to him because I honoured him, and you must give your honour to him because I honoured him to be My deputy. Prostrate to him!"

All of the angels prostrated. But Satan said, "No. I like democracy" [laughs]. "This is not justice!" shouting at Allah. *Utanmaz, Şeytan, namussuz pesave!*[5] Not accepting, saying, "No, this is not right! We must have an election, we must use democracy. Must be democracy! Democracy—you don't know democracy? *That* we must do! Bring boxes to put everyone's votes. Then I will come to be on that throne."

---

[5][Tr.,] Shameless Satan, dishonourable scoundrel.

Then Allah Almighty said, "Demon, go away! You are Shaytan. In front of My Divine Presence, from where are you getting the courage to say to Me, 'You are wrong'? You are cursed! Go away, demon!"[6]

At that time, he was asking for democracy. Now, everywhere [parodies], "Democracy is best, democracy is best!"

This is an analysis of democracy that no one knows. Yes? Americans, Germans and Cypriots, Turks, Arabs. *"Wailu lil-'Arab,"*[7] never understanding anything about the Holy Qur'an. All of them, Arabs, are running after democracy, democratic *nizam*, system, and they are saying, "We are Muslims." And also Iranians. They are claiming, "We are first class Muslims," making a parliament because a parliament must be in democratic countries—those *Shi'ah*, who are claiming, "We would die for *Ahl al-Bait*, the holy family of *Rasul-Allah*."[8] The holy family of *Rasul-Allah* ﷺ is calling you to democracy, to parliament? And Pakistani people, also, they are saying, "No one can be Muslims like us."

They have lost the way, while they are claiming to have a democratic system. Where is it written in holy books? In the Old Testament or New Testament or Holy Qur'an, where is it written? The Old Testament, New Testament—all are saying "kings, kings, kings." They have lost it, and their claims are false.

---

[6] 2:30-34, 7:13, 15:34-35, 38:77-78.

[7] Woe to the Arabs!

[8] The Messenger of Allah.

Therefore, this world can't reach a good end till they bring their *sultans*, their kings, and kick out tyrants and democracy. Monarchy must come, must come! If not, they will kill each other till this world goes from six billion to one billion. Democracy is bringing that big punishment to them. Those who quickly come to Allah Almighty's way, they should be saved. Others are going to finish and vanish.

May Allah forgive us! Correct your minds, O people, all the world's people! This is not addressed only to the handful people in front of me, but I am calling all people to think about it deeply, to know Reality and to accept Reality, and to come the way of Allah Almighty.

May Allah forgive me and bless those who accept truth. For the honour of the most honoured one in His Divine Presence, Sayyidina. Muhammad ﷺ—*Fateha!* ▲

3

CONCERNING THE EVILS OF THIS TIME

A'udhu bil-Lahi min ash-Shaytani-r-rajeem. Bismillahi-r-Rahmani-r-Raheem. La hawla wa la quwwata illa bil-Lahi-l-'Aliyi-l-'Azheem.

We are asking from our Lord, the Lord of Heavens, our Creator, Allah Almighty, for the honour of the most honoured one in His Divine Presence, Sayyidina Muhammad ﷺ, to give us good understanding. Good understanding brings peace, but misunderstandings bring troubles because misunderstandings make people do wrong things.

If you let your donkey,[1] it will never go on the road, always wanting to run on the land. Its happiness is to be on the land, in meadows. But if you train your donkey, it may follow your way. If not, it will always leave the right way and run to wrong ways.

And if you leave people without guidance, they will always follow the wrong way. Therefore, Allah Almighty is

---

[1] A metaphor for ego *[nafs]*.

saying, "You must have a control system for controlling people. When they leave the right way, you must look and control what they do—whether they are doing good things, following a good way, or following a wrong way."

That must be, a heavenly order: Don't leave people without control! You must control them. That must be! But now that mu'assasah, foundation, has gone. Governments are not taking care of their people, saying, "Everyone is free." Yes, everyone is free! Then, if anyone does something wrong, taking him, putting him in court and punishing him, sending him to jail.

That is not a correct way. It is nonsense, it is ignorance, to leave people till they do a wrong thing and then take them away. Governments' rules allow people to do everything wrong and then catch them. No! That is our mind-product. The Lord of Heavens wants to prevent people from doing wrong things, but governments, no. Governments are saying, "We make so many rules. If anyone does any wrong thing, we will punish him."

No. That is the difference between heavenly rules and people's rules. Democracy, that we are calling *"pocracy,"*[2] is the dirtiest system, giving people unlimited freedom. You can do anything! But heavenly rules, the alternative to democracy, is theocracy. Those heavenly rules teach people and control their actions, not leaving them to do a wrong thing or go on the wrong way.[3] Those are heavenly rules,

---

[2] Literally "ruling system of manure".

[3] That is, a divine system of rules preventing offenses or harm in contrast to a man-made system that leaves people free to offend or experience harm and then punishes them or tries too late to mend the situation.

and democratic rules have no value. Therefore, democracy is a wholly wrong way.

And Satan is doing the biggest advertising and saying, "You must use democracy." For what? Now the whole world is falling into bottomless troubles, unlimited, unsolvable problems, and governments don't know how they can deal with people, or people, how they are going to deal with governments. And each day I am hearing that there is *intikhab*, election: election in Turkey; election in Germany; election in France; election in Italy; election . . .

Whom are you electing? The same people, the same quality of people. A hundred times you are bringing the same heads to be in power, nothing changing. And they are saying, "O people, look! *You* are governing your country because you have elected and brought these people from among yourselves." And people are saying, "We are never happy with such people," but by force they are putting them.

Allah Almighty closes the doors of wrong ways, putting barriers, saying, "Stop! You can't go from this way."

Others are saying, "No, no barrier." A barrier keeps people from falling down. The government says, democracy says, "No, no barrier. You can go." And perhaps that bridge is broken. "Doesn't matter. Let them fall! They are free." But Allah Almighty says, "No. There is danger and you must keep yourself away.

Therefore, this is now the time of tyrants, as the Prophet ﷺ was saying—the period of tyrants, everywhere tyrants.[4] They are not looking at holy books, they are not obeying heavenly orders and commands. All of them are on the wrong way, and daily more curses are coming on them, till you ask, "O our Lord, take them away! Send from your sincere, good servants to take them away, those deceivers, those tyrants, and to save Your servants." They are taking over everything, never leaving. But the time is over now!

Now, because governments are not taking any care of heavenly rules, wanting to make rules by themselves, troubles are increasing. And we are trying to make people keep heavenly rules by themselves because everywhere, the people who should be responsible, as a shepherd protects his flocks from wolves, from violent wild animals, have been lost. No shepherds now. Without a shepherd, people are running like this, like that, and falling into the hands of wolves, and they are suffering, suffering. Everywhere people are suffering, and that is the sign of the Last Days.

And Shaytan is urging people to run in wrong directions. They are saying,[5] "You must learn!" What are they learning? The ways of Shaytan. Everywhere, educational systems are calling people to learn the ways of Shaytan and to fall into troubles, and problems are increasing and no solutions for problems, countless problems.

---

[4]The Prophet (s) said, "After me come caliphs, and after the caliphs come princes, and after princes there will be kings and after the kings, there will be tyrants." (Na 'im bin Hamad)

[5]Governments and educational systems.

First of all, people must learn and must take care of the command of the Lord of Heavens. You must take it and you must look, you must understand. But first, democratic educational systems are teaching people *not* to say there is a Lord, there is a Creator, there is God, there is Allah Almighty. They are first denying God, and they are establishing their teaching systems on atheistic theories.

From where is that terrorism coming? On every product there is written,, "Made in England" or "Made in Germany," "Made in Holland," "Made in Italy." "Made in Argentina—no. Something, "Made in Turkey," "Made in Greece"? "Made in Arabia"? No, I don't know. "Made in China." They are saying China is like a big dragon, wanting to eat, to swallow Western countries, and they are trembling now.

Hah-hah! Like Yajuj-Majuj.[6] One kind of them are Chinese people, Mongol people, and most Asian people and Turkish people. Yajuj-Majuj, Gog-Magog are the sons of Yapheth.[7] Hami, Sami and Yapheth: Sami, Arabs; Hami, Europeans; and Yapheth's children are Turks, Chinese, Mongols, Japanese, and also Malaysians and such people—Gog-Magog, all of them. I don't know about Americans; they are new ones. Who is their father? I don't know. But they are a combination of some of Ham's and Yapheth's children. They are very happy. Yes? Any American here?

---

[6]Ya'juj wa Ma'juj, an unidentified race of people mentioned in the Qur'an, 18:94, 97-98; 21:95-96.
[7]Yapeth=Jafeth; Hami=Ham; Sami=Shem.

And now all these nations aren't able to do anything, and they are falling into bottomless darkness. They aren't able to find the way. Even if they have a compass, maps, it is darkness. People need a light. And the light that they are asking for is not the light of the sun. It is the light of faith, the light of beliefs. Belief in Allah makes their way clear to move, to go on.

But now the whole world has just extinguished the lights of religions. People do not believe in anything and they are in darkness. That is the problem, the biggest problem. Everywhere, that darkness of ignorance is rejecting everything that belongs to Heavens. And we are asking from Allah Almighty to send us, from His Divine Presence, those who will bring lights (and their lights are much more powerful than the light of the sun), to show people what is wrong and what is right. Otherwise, people now aren't able to see, to know, what is wrong, what is true, what is right.

Only *ahad un-nass*,[8] certain people, are trying to find a way with their candles. Candles are so weak for finding a way but still they are helping people a little bit. But the majority is in dark darkness. It is out of our capacity to stop it; ordinary people aren't able to stop it. It needs heavenly intervention to come on earth and make people see and know what is right, what is wrong.

Individually, some people are trying to do that. They are doing it only in their homes, but when they go out it is so difficult. What their, our, children are taking from their parents in their homes, that small candle, when they go out, windy storms are extinguishing and they are falling into

---

[8]Certain, special people.

darkness. And the Prophet ☺ was saying, "O people, guard your youngsters." It is only one sentence, but it may change the lives of people if they follow it. He was saying, "O mankind, O people, O servants of the Lord, keep your youngsters at home after sunset. Don't let them go outside."⁹

It is enough to change the whole world, this command only: *"Don't let them go out after sunset. Keep them in your homes."* Finished, because after sunset it is the time of *intisharu-l-jinn*;¹⁰ the time of jinn and shaytans. They are free, running in the streets, everywhere. Therefore, keep your children from going out. Otherwise, they may fall into the hands of shaytans and jinns; finished. Look! No need for anything else.

At nighttime, keep them at home. Leave the streets empty. Night clubs, casinos, *eglence yeri*,¹¹ playing places or enjoyment places that draw youngsters to them—finished! They should be shut down. Finished, finished! Then the whole world may be in silence, in good condition, so that every one may feel satisfaction at that time. Only one command from the Seal of the Prophets, and it right, just giving proof of that command. Holy books, the Old Testament, New Testament and Psalms, also, they are saying don't leave your youngsters outside after sunset. Keep them at home—finished!

---

⁹ *Altaqitoo subyanikum awwal al-'isha fa innahu waqt intishar ash-shayatin.*

¹⁰The spreading out or diffusion of jinn.

¹¹[Tr.,] places of entertainment.

And another command: Don't bring what is happening outside into your homes. It is also a big *fitna*,[12] a big trouble, coming now from that shaytanic box, TV, bringing everything happening outside into your home, and they are learning everything through that, even if they do not go out.

Close it down, also. But Shaytan is keeping it;, and he is also making some foolish people to destroy, to make bombs and kill innocent people, so that Allah curses them. They should find their punishment before they leave this life!

Close down TVs after *Maghrib*, after sunset. And use it for some useful purpose. Don't bring what is happening outside into your home to teach your youngsters every bad, every satanic thing. The biggest satanic school, that is the TV studios. May Allah take them away!

For the honour of the most honoured one in His Divine Presence, Sayyidina Muhammad ﷺ—*Fateha!* ▲

---

[12]Trial, enticement, temptation, fascination.

4

ALIVE HEARTS, DEAD HEARTS

A'udhu bil-Lahi min ash-Shaytani-r-rajeem. Bismillahi-r-Rahmani-r-Raheem. La hawla wa la quwatta illa bil-Lahi-l-'Aliyyi-l-'Azheem.[1]

We are asking forgiveness from Allah Almighty, because I am looking at myself and at all people, and I am not seeing a person walking on the right way.

It is a pity that people are going in a dangerous direction, although it is written, "Paradise Way, Hells Way." But people are running on the wrong way, in a dangerous direction, heedlessly, and to be heedless brings every trouble to people. Wrong step, and after it there is going to be a punishment.

With every step that a person takes on the wrong way, there quickly reaches him a punishment. They may say, "I do not feel anything." That is an admission that they are heedless, not understanding what is happening to them

---

[1] "I take refuge with Allah from Satan, the rejected. In the name of Allah, the Beneficent, the Merciful. There is no might nor power except with Allah, the Most High, the Almighty."

when they walk on the wrong way. At the least, the Prophet ﷺ was saying, any wrong step, wrong action, makes a black spot on our hearts till our hearts are going to die. When it is completely black, black spots coming, coming, coming, then our hearts are going to die, finished.

"Dying" means that no more lights are reaching our hearts, and the life of our hearts is heavenly lights. Heavenly lights are making your heart be alive. And the Prophet ﷺ was also saying that if a person keeps his steps on the right path, in the right direction, a safe direction, when other people's hearts are dying, his heart is never going to die because lights are coming to those who walk on the right path, and lights make our hearts alive. When lights are cut off, we are going to die.

"O Shaykh, we see so many billions of people, running, going and coming, going and coming. They say that they are alive."

No, no. Really, they have died. It is not a real life when divine lights never enter and every wrong step makes a black spot on their hearts, their hearts becoming a black piece. Finished—that is hearts' "dying". And when people fall into darkness, fear comes on them. They are afraid, as a person in darkness never feels safe, never sees what is coming on him in the dark, and he is afraid. When lights are on, that fear leaves him.

Therefore, those whose hearts are alive, they are in satisfaction and contentment. And the engine that gives hearts lights, that is *dhikr*,² the remembrance of Allah, to be with Allah. Those who are making *dhikr*, they are with Allah, and Allah gives power to their hearts. That is real life for hearts, and those who never make *dhikr* in their hearts, they have died.

Those who are with Allah are never going to die. Allah Almighty's existence is never-ending; His existence is from pre-eternity to post-eternity. And when His divine lights come into the hearts of servants, servants are also going to reach that real life because when those divine lights, come, you will become *hayy*, living ones forever.

Once a shaykh passed away from this temporary life. Everyone is going to pass. And they buried the shaykh. And his *murid*³ was inside the grave to arrange the shaykh's position, and he was thinking that the shaykh was like an ordinary person.

No! A real shaykh must be extraordinary, as prophets are from mankind but they are extraordinary beings, and their inheritors, also, are not like ordinary or common people. No; must be higher. They may be at the same level in their physical being but their spiritual being is above the level of common people. If not, a person can't be a shaykh, he can't be a guide. A guide must look, must see [the needs and inner being of] common people.

---

²*Dhikr-Allah, zikr,* the remembrance or mention of Allah through audible or silent recitation of Qur'anic verses, His Holy Names, and well-known litanies of glorification.

³The disciple or follower of a shaykh.

That *murid* knew that the *Shari'ah*⁴ says that when a person is buried in his grave, you must turn his face towards *qiblah*, towards the House of the Lord, the Ka'bah,⁵ and he was trying to do that. But the shaykh opened his eyes and said, "O *waladi*,⁶ O my *murid*, no need for you to turn my face towards *qiblah*. *He* has turned my face to Himself. No need!"

And that *murid* was so frightened, and he said, "O our master, you are not dead! How are we burying you?"

He said, "O my son, those who are with Allah, they do not die. Our lives are continuous. You are only making a veil that we have passed away. When our time in this life is over, we pass behind the veil and leave you, and we are now behind the veil. In only one step, we have passed there. You finish your job. Cover me; don't talk too much. Make my grave like other people's and go."

Yes, those people's hearts are alive! If hearts are alive, their lives have just passed from the imitation, temporary life to the permanent life, to infinity. Their lives are continuous, nothing causing them to be broken.

Therefore, guard your heart. Allah Almighty says, *"Ala bi dhikri-Allahi tatmainu-l-qulub.*⁷ Your hearts may reach real satisfaction and contentment when you are with Me. When

---

⁴The sacred Law of Islam, derived primarily from the Holy Qur'an and the Prophet's practice *(Sunnah)*.

⁵*Qiblah:* the direction of Mecca from any part of the globe. *Ka'bah,* the Sacred House in Mecca that all Muslims face during their prayers, built in antiquity by the prophet Abraham and his son, the prophet Ishmael,.

⁶"O my son."

⁷*"Unquestionably, by the remembrance of Allah hearts are assured."* (13:28)

you say *'Allah!'* you are with Me. But when you forget Me, you are not with Me, no. You are thrown away, you are going to be dust. You have lost those lights, you have lost that honour of being with Me."

No honour can be above that honour of being with Allah; no honour can be given to servants more than being with their Lord. But most people have lost it because they are giving importance only their temporary life and physical desires that are going to finish and vanish. They are not running after real life, to reach divine lights.

When people go on the right path, at every moment divine lights reach them, and at every moment their hope, their satisfaction, their pleasure, their enjoyment increases, becoming more and more. Fear leaves them and they are full of hope, and their hope is real hope. Their hope is to reach more and more in the Divine Presence, Allah Almighty's never-ending favours and never-ending pleasures from Him to His servants. Then their hearts are alive, with no black spot on them.

And try—try! Don't sleep! Try to reach real life *here*. But you can't walk with wrong steps to real life. You need correct steps to reach such favors, the endless Favors Oceans, endless Pleasure Oceans, endless enjoyments, endless Mercy Oceans, endless Blessing Oceans of Allah Almighty, never becoming less but "*Wa ladayna mazid,*[8] always more and more, never less.

But those who are running after their physical being's enjoyments, day by day they become less, less, less, and finishing. When their hearts are completely black, they are fin-

---

[8]*"And with Us there is more."* (50:35)

ished. They may walk, they may eat, they may see but enjoyment has just finished, no more taste. They may eat but no taste; they may look but they can't enjoy through their looking; they may go and come but they never reach any good feeling of pleasure. Their lives' pleasures are just finished. They are really dead.

When you look at them, you think that that is an ordinary person, but they are finished. They are finished, everything becoming less, less, less; no taste, no enjoyment, no more response from their physical being for enjoying themselves—finished! They are living dead people; they are waiting for the time to be taken away from their physical being and be buried—finished!

But those whose hearts are alive, their physical being is also enjoying. They never lose their taste. Eating, drinking, looking, going, coming—their enjoyment never goes away because of their spiritual power, and their enjoyment is more than young people's. Young people think their enjoyment is at the top level. No! They may be ninety years old, those people who are with Allah, but what they taste, also, through their physical being, young people can't reach. And till they leave this life, jumping to real life from this temporary life, they never lose anything of physical powers, also.

If people knew that secret of *tariqats*,[9] all of them would run to *tariqats*. But Shaytan is making them not to believe and to deny *tariqats*, the way of *dhikr*—and the way of *dhikr*

---

[9]Sufi orders.

is to be with Allah Almighty. Shaytan is preventing them and saying it is something forbidden.[10]

Dhikr forbidden? They are saying, "Yes!" Go to Makkatu-l-Mukarramah[11] now and say *"La ilaha illa-Llah"*[12] with ten people, and police will come and take you away.

"What are you doing?"

"What am I doing? I am saying *'La ilaha illa-Lah.'*"

"No, you can't say it!"

People now are in such a way, even in Makkat-l-Mukarramah, Madinatu-l-Munawwarah.[13] If you say, "As-

---

[10] That is, by the Wahabi religious authorities, who emphasize a rationalist understanding of Islam.

[11] Mecca the Honoured/Venerated.

[12] The first clause of the Islamic Declaration of Faith, "There is no deity except Allah." Repeating it in a group is falsely regarded as being a Sufi practice, and hence it is frowned upon by the Wahabi religious authorities, despite the fact that it was done by the Prophet and his *Sahabah*, as reported in the following *hadith*, narrated by Ya'la bin Shaddad:

> My father reported and said, while 'Ubada bin Samit ؓ was present and confirmed it: We were with the Prophet ﷺ and he asked, "Is there any stranger among you." We said, "No, O Messenger of Allah." He ordered us to close the door and said, "Raise your hands and say *'La ilaha illa-Llah,'*" whereupon we raised our hands, [doing so] for an hour. Then he said, *"Alhamdulillah!* O Allah, You have sent me with this word and have empowered me thereby, and have promised me Paradise because of it, and You never fail in Your promise." He then said, "Shall I not give you the good tidings that indeed Allah has forgiven you?" (Ahmad)

[13] Medina the Radiant, the city that was the Prophet's home during the last period of his life and in which he is buried..

salat was-salam 'alaika, ya Rasul-Allah,"[14] police will come and say, "You can't say this. He is dead."

How, "dead"? The Prophet ﷺ went and visited *shuhada Uhud*, the martyrs of Uhud,[15] and said, *"As-salamu 'alaikum, ya shuhada', ya ghuraba', wa rahmat-Allahi wa barakatuhu."*[16] He gave *salam*.[17] But now people in Madinatu-l-Munawwarah are saying, "You can't say this to the Prophet," although the Prophet himself said it while visiting Jannat al-Baqi, Jannat al-Mu'alla.[18]

How, from where, did you bring this barrier? How are you banning people from visiting the graves of *awliya*, of *Sahabah*,[19] and destroying their graves? What is this foolishness and disrespect? "I am here and you are coming and

---

[14]"Blessings and peace be on you, O Messenger of Allah." According to the Wahhabi understanding, greeting the Prophet at his grave in Medina constitutes *shirk* (attributing divinity to other than Allah) because, according to their understanding, the Prophet is dead, despite the fact that it is stated in a *hadith* that Allah has prohibited the earth from consuming the bodies of prophets. Traditional Islamic belief, on the other hand, holds that Muhammad and all the prophets are alive in their graves, separated from the 'living' by a spiritual veil. Moreover, as taught by the Prophet himself, Muslims throughout the world send this greeting to the Prophet multiple times a day during their prayers *(salat)*, and, according to his own words, he hears and responds.

[15]The second battle between the polytheists of Mecca and the Muslims, which took place near Medina.

[16]"Peace be upon you, O martyrs, O departed ones, and the mercy of Allah and His blessings."

[17]The Islamic greeting of peace.

[18]The burial places of the martyrs of the Prophet's time

[19]The Companions of the Prophet, including the martyrs who died in battle against the idolaters.

destroying my place on my head!" That is respect? May Allah take them away, quickly! Yes.

Try to follow the steps of *awliya* as much as you can. Walk in their steps and you should be happy here and Hereafter, and no fear for you here or Hereafter. May Allah forgive us! For the honour of the most honoured one in His Divine Presence, Sayyidina Muhammad ﷺ—*Fateha!*

If *awliya's* pleasure were given to all people, they would be drunk. *Their* enjoyment is material, but *awliya's* pleasure is spiritual. Materiality will finish, but spirituality is never-ending, every time, every time. They are not in need of using anything to eat, to drink. ▲

5

THE IMPORTANCE OF LEARNING GOOD SERVANTHOOD

A'udhu bil-Lahi min ash-Shaytani-r-rajeem. Bismillahi-r-Rahmani-r-Raheem. La hawla wa la quwwata illa bil-Lahi-l-'Aliyi-l-'Azheem.

By the name of Allah, All-Mighty, All-Merciful, Most Beneficent and Most Munificent. It is an Association[1] with the shaykh, and we are in need to listen and to obey. And, as we have been created, we have been given responsibility for certain important things.

Nothing is created without a wisdom or without a purpose or without a benefit. Everything, from the smallest particle of creation—an atom, you may say—is created for some purpose.

An atom can be divided into smaller particles. You can't say that even the smallest particle of matter is created

---

[1] Ar., *suhbah;* Tr., *sohbet,* meaning a time of gathering and association of the shaykh with his followers *(murids).*

without a reason. Allah Almighty says, *"Rabbana. ma khalaqta hadha batilan,"*² teaching us. You must say, "O my Lord, this was not created without a purpose." And when it is created with some purpose, Allah creating and giving that speciality to all things, some benefit must be granted to mankind.

Everything is created with some wisdoms and purposes. For what, for what? Did Allah create creation—the earth, planets, galaxies, countless, unlimited spaces—for Himself? If you think in such a way, that is the biggest mistake in your beliefs.

Allah, the Lord of Heavens, the Creator of everything, is not in need of anything. If He were in need of something, He couldn't be the Creator, He couldn't be the Lord of Heavens; no. He created everything, but He is not in need, even of such huge spaces and distances in space as astronauts are seeing, and they are saying, "Space—we can't measure it, even with as many numbers as possible. We may put a huge number, but it is not enough to measure distances in space." We may say that maybe you can find a number to reach the farthest galaxy, but you can't reach deeper into space. Space is unlimited, but everything in it is within limits.

Therefore, He is not the Creator to be needy. *He* created; *He* gives existence to creation. How can He be in need of what He created? He gives creation whatever *it* may be in need of. How can you think that He may be in need of these huge universes? No! It is outside of intellect; mind and mental faculties can never accept that. "I bring that into ex-

---

² *"Our Lord, You did not create this in vain."* (3:191)

istence and I expect some benefit from it for Myself"—how can it be? Wrong way, wrong idea, wrong thinking about the Lord of Heavens!

But people now in the twenty-first century are not thinking about it. They are trying to make the Creator according to their imagination. If you say, "Allah is the Creator," they ask, *"How—how* is He?" And this question that they are asking, "How is He?" is a nonsensical question because, if you want to put that question, it means that you want to bring Him into your area of imagination, that you think the Creator's identity is like our identities.

Therefore, asking, *"How* is Allah, *how* is God? Where is He? How is He?" is the biggest mistake because they want to put Him in their area of imagination, like a person wanting to see a ceremony that is taking place in London or in America or in Germany, and he is looking at the TV screen. Yes; he wants to look at that thirty or forty centimeters' space, saying, "Oh, this is the Queen, this is the King, this is the parade. This is a gigantic aircraft, this is the battlefield. This is Baghdad, this is London."

You may bring that on that TV screen and say such foolish things, such as, "We must see Him." Where? On the TV screen? What is that foolishness? Where can you see Him? I may say to that person, "What you are asking for, if you can reach beyond space, you may find Him there. Try to reach!"

Mars is the nearest planet to our earth. What about beyond that? You can't reach the nearest planet in our solar system, and our solar system is only one star in our galaxy. And they say that in 120,000 light years you may reach the edge of this galaxy. And beyond that—how are you asking to reach beyond that, beyond that, and then reaching empty space and going in it, to finish? You can't finish space.

Where is He, where is He? *Where?* There is a *tamthil*, an example. Some small fishes are saying to their mother, "We hear that there is an ocean. O mother, show us where it is." And the mother is saying, "O my little ones, show me anywhere that there is *not* ocean."

That is an ocean, and billions and billions of galaxies are swimming in it. No one knows from where they have come, no one knows to where they reach. But foolishness has just reached the top point in the twenty-first century because they want to deny, and they are never using their minds or mental faculties, asking to bring Allah on the TV screen. *Allahu Akbar!*

He created everything! He is the Creator and He is not in need of anything. And He is only one. Can't be a second one; no room for another Creator. Two creators can't be. One must be a creature. One, only one Creator, but countless creations and creatures.

Foolishness from people concerning their Creator! They are taking it as *istikhfaf*,[3] making it not important. "It is not important to ask about the Creator."

"Why?"

"Because we are busy on earth, we are busy! No time for us to think about the Creator. We are so busy! Twenty-

---

[3]Lightly, frivolously, as if unimportant.

four hours is not enough for our works, for our business, for our job. We are so busy. No time!"

[Chuckles.] Sometimes they put watches one hour ahead. I am saying, "People want to make the day twenty-five hours?" They are thinking about it. They are saying, "Twenty-four hours is not enough for our works. What can we do? In summertime, we can put it one hour forward. And when we are tired of summertime, twenty-five hours. In wintertime, take it back one hour, twenty-three hours." [Laughter.] They are really asking to make a longer day, to make our day forty-eight hours. And if it were to be forty-eight hours, we would say, "Oh! We are fed up with long days, long nights. We must bring it back as it was"—yes.

Twenty four hours is just suitable but people think that they have such big activities, big business and big works that they are in. "We see that there is not enough time to think beyond our works about Allah. No time for us to ask about the Creator because we are so busy. Twenty-four hours we are busy with *dunya*.[4] No time to ask for *Maula*, Allah!"

When are you going to be free, unoccupied, or when are you going to be retired? I am asking. "Are you *re*tired or tired?" Tired, because if not tired, no one would be retired. Retired means finished, finished. "I am tired. I ran so quickly that now I need to rest." Yes; after a while you can find your rest in the grave, full rest there.

The twenty-first century's people, they are busy. They are saying, "No time for praying, no time to think about Heavens or heavenly beings. No time! We are, all of us, just

---

[4]The world, worldly affairs.

occupied." And that brings them endless troubles and unsolved problems because they are not thinking about their Creator, the Lord of Heavens. "Twenty-four hours," they are saying, "it is not enough for our business, and we have no time."

And everywhere from East to West, from North to South, that you are finding troubles and problems, that is the reason. If sitting and saying, "Oh, *alhamdulillah!*[5] Now, O our Lord, I am asking to be with You. If I am with You, I am feeling satisfaction and peace within myself. If not, I am not in peace or in satisfaction."

Therefore, *Sahabah*, may Allah bless them, made *dunya* their last goal, and they kept as their first goal to reach the pleasure of their Lord, Allah Almighty. When you make Allah Almighty pleased with you, He makes everything easy for you. When you leave Him and forget, everything is going to be more of a burden on you and you may waste all your energy, and finally you will reach nothing. *Hasiluhu*[6]— when putting numbers and making a line under them, what comes? They are making everything under that line come to zero, zero, zero, zero, zero. Their lives are ending with zero. They are losing their chance here and Hereafter—*khasira-d-dunya wal-akhirat*,[7] from both sides.

At the beginning, we were saying that an atom or less, something smaller than an atom, is never created without a reason. Through heavenly knowledge, traditional

---

[5]All praise is for Allah.
[6]Its sum total.
[7]*"He has lost[both] this world and the Hereafter."* (22:11)

knowledge that was granted to the prophets, we know that everything is created for man and that man represents the Lord of Heavens—the *khalifah*,[8] representative of Allah on earth. Therefore, everything is created to be in His service for you, everything should help you and serve you. That is the honour of being the representative of Allah Almighty.

What about yourself? Everything is a servant to you. The wisdom of their creation is that Allah Almighty filled every place with countless creatures, only for *you*.

It is a prison, this world, but Allah Almighty has also made such beautiful decorations in nature so that His servants will not feel that they are in prison and will be happy to do divine service here and to be deputies. When they learn servanthood and leave this prison, they are going to be in His Divine Presence, servants in His divine service.

This is the preparation for being there, but people have lost it because Shaytan and shaytanic teachings are saying, "Don't listen! Come with me! I shall show you how you can enjoy yourself, I shall teach you about an enjoyable life. Come with me!" And people are running after that and falling into troubles.

Keep yourself with your Lord's service. *That* is first. You must do this. You may feel satisfaction in your heart and refreshment in your physical being, always going to be in power. You may always taste; you can't lose the taste of a good life. You may taste every favor that is granted to you in nature, not changing even if you are ninety or a hundred

---

[8]Caliph; deputy, vicegerent.

years old. But those who do not look after that, their taste becomes less, less, less, less.

If you give someone honey, he may say, "What is it? No taste, this."

"This is honey."

"I don't think it is honey. It is such a bitter thing. No, I am not tasting it."

Anything that he ate and drank and enjoyed before, you may give it to him and say, "Take it, take it, take it!"

"How can you eat this? No taste!" because Allah Almighty takes that good feeling from them because they are servants of Shaytan—taking it away, and everything they eat is like ashes, no taste, or like straw. If eating straw, what? Nothing!

O people, come to Allah! O people, come to way of Allah if you want to be happy here and Hereafter, to be in peace. If not, *you know!*

What shall we do? Everyone is just buried in his grave. But now there are so many people, also, and it is not for everyone to find a private grave. Hundreds of people are put in a *khandaq*,[9] a big place. They are digging and putting everyone, one on top of another, in such a way.

O people, keep yourselves and fight against Shaytan, fight his teachings! Come to the teachings of prophets, particularly the Seal of Prophets, Sayyidina Muhammad ﷺ.

---

[9] Trench, hole.

WE HAVE HONORED THE CHILDREN OF ADAM

May Allah forgive me and bless you! For the honour of the most honoured one in His Divine Presence, Sayyidina Muhammad ﷺ—*Fateha!* ▲

6

KEEPING RESPECT FOR ALL OF ALLAH'S SERVANTS

A'udhu bil-Lahi min ash-Shaytani-r-rajeem. Bismillahi-r-Rahmani-r-Raheem. La hawla wa la quwwata illa bil-Lahi-l-'Aliyi-l-'Azheem.

This is not a good seating for me, but I am trying to take my rest.[1]. And I am asking forgiveness and apologizing that I am sitting in such a way in front of you.

Real, true Islam came to show people their value. If prophets had not come, no one would know the value of mankind. And now people have lost the value of mankind, and when they lose the value of mankind, they also lose respect for each other.

Allah created men and He, Almighty, honoured them. That means that He gives respect to that extraordinary or

---

[1] During this *sohbet*, due to a foot ailment, Shaykh Nazim was obliged to sit with his feet toward the gathering, which is contrary to Islamic manners.

most distinguished creature. Throughout all creation, the most valuable, most honoured one, is mankind.² That means that Allah Almighty gives His respect to them.

Therefore, He ordered the angels to make *sajdah*, to prostrate to Adam. That is the utmost limit of respect. Prostrating, making *sajdah*, is only for Allah; but He ordered the angels to prostrate to Adam, saying, "I just honoured this new one, new creature, and I am giving My respect and honour and blessings to him. Beware not to be disrespectful to his kind. You must respect mankind!"

The angels were saying, "O our Lord, why are You going to make a *khalifah* on earth? They are going to be first-class trouble-makers on earth, killing one another, doing every badness, every wildness, violence, but you are giving that honour to them! Let that honour be for us."

Allah was saying, "No, no. You don't know. I know! I am not in need of you to remind Me. I know! Don't say such a thing again! I know what I am doing, I know about what I am creating. I know that they have such a characteristic, but even so, I am making them My representatives and deputies on earth. Prostrate to him!"

Shaytan was saying, "Oh, no! I am not making *sajdah*. Democracy! [Laughter.] Let the angels tell if they are saying 'Yes' for Adam or for me. Must be election, democracy!"

The first democracy, there. He was saying to Allah, "I am not accepting such a thing from You, no. We must do an election or a referendum. If people say Adam is suitable, I will be happy. If not, *I* must be that one." And he was say-

---

²"*And We have certainly honoured the children of Adam.*" (17:70)

ing within himself, "Even if the referendum comes out for him, I am not going to accept that. I am going to say 'No!'"

Allah was saying, "Demon! *Jahannama git! Yakıl!*³ Who are you to speak in My Divine Presence, to say this? I am making that one the king over you. *I* am giving that honour. You *can't* give honour!"⁴

Therefore, democracy is *batil*.⁵ Honour is given to people by Heavens, not by common people making a president, prime minister, this, that. Whomever Allah gives respect and honour to, you must respect him. All creation respects man, mankind, and only the twenty-first century's people are not giving respect to each other, making the value of man less than a mouse, less than a small creature. They are saying [parodies], "Animal rights," some foolish people making such claims, saying, "Oh, we must keep the rights of animals."

There are no rights for mankind? We are making men like garbage, killing; not asking about their rights but asking about rights for animals? Allah is saying, "Rights of animals—yes, they have rights, but the rights of mankind, *that* is important."

Nations are not giving respect to other nations. Even among themselves, among their citizens, among their own peoples, they are not giving the respect with which Allah is respecting mankind. That is the sources of troubles and fighting now.

---

³[Tr.,] "Go to Hell! Burn!"
⁴The story of the creation of Adam and Satan's rebellion is contained in 2:30-34.
⁵False, baseless, vain, futile.

We Have Honored the Children of Adam

I am coming to this point because I am putting my feet towards you, and it is not a respectful way of sitting. Because Allah respects you, I must respect you; everyone must respect others. That is Islam! No fundamentalists, no terrorists, no such groups of people, trouble-makers, radical groups. If anything happens, explosion, they say, "*We* have done this."

That is not Islam, no. Allah should ask them, should punish them! *La darar wa la dirara fil-Islam.*[6] It is something that must be written in golden letters, to be hung everywhere. Islam prevents harming people or doing harm, Allah preventing it and saying, "Don't go and harm him—no."

No harming in Islam! Islam keeps respect for everyone. Particularly, Islam is careful about non-Muslims who are living with us,[7] to keep their rights, not to touch them, not to harm them; because it is such a serious thing on the Day of Resurrection. Allah is saying, "You may take from him as much as he harmed you, not keeping your rights. Now take the same from him.[8] Give him his rights!" But finished! People are not taking any care, and Islam just came to keep *sharaf ul-insan*, the honour of mankind.

---

[6]"There is no harming or being harmed in Islam." <u>Muwatta</u> Malik, <u>Mustadrak</u> of Hakim.

[7]That is, through rules enjoining good treatment of non-Muslim minorities living in Muslim lands *(dhimmis)*, particularly with regard to their places of worship and practice of religion.

[8]Referring to 5:45/5:48 in Yusuf Ali's translation.

Anzilu-n-nassa manazilahum[9]; give all people their honour according to their level. And to bring the lowest level person to the highest level is also forbidden because his level is the first level. You can't bring him to the top level, and this democracy may take the lowest level person to be in the highest position. That is *batil*. But Muslims—no minds now; everyone is misunderstanding! No more good-understanding people among Muslims, finished.

Respect! *"Wa la tansa'u-l-fadla bainakum"*;[10] you must give the proper value among yourselves. "This is a teacher, this is a professor." Don't treat that one like a student. There must be a line of respect between you; he must be an honoured one. At home, women must give their respect to their husbands; children must give their respect to parents; younger ones must give their respect to older ones—in such a way. That is the essence of Islam.

Islam just came to give honour, or *iyada*,[11] to give back, the respect that people had lost from the time of *Jahiliyah*, the Period of Ignorance.[12] *Badu*,[13] Arabs, they never gave any care or respect to poor people, to women, to weak ones, to old ones, to servants, to slaves. They only gave it to those who were powerful and filled their pockets with gold. To them they gave respect; to others, no. Therefore, Islam came to give back everyone's espect. And everyone should be respected at his or her level because Allah Almighty made,

---

[9]"Give people the respect due their station." Sahih Muslim
[10]*"And do not forget precedence among yourselves."* (2:237)
[11]Revert to, reinstate, re-establish, bring back.
[12]The era of ignorance of divine guidance among the Arabs prior to Islam.
[13]Bedouins.

also, so many levels. Those people must be on their levels, to give respect to the high-level people—the high-level people who are carrying the responsibility of the whole nation, of the whole *ummah*.[14]

It is not just being a top-level person. If reaching the highest position, the highest level, there is also loaded on his shoulders a heavy responsibility. He should be asked about his nation, about his people, in the Divine Presence, if he gave the rights of those that he was over. And Shaytan, for thousands of years, has always tried to divide people into two groups, powerful ones and weak ones, and powerful ones never showed any respect or kindness or mercy to weak ones. Islam came and gave everyone's rights. And the weakest ones are going to be the most powerful ones with regard to their rights.

The state must look after weak ones, not after powerful ones; no. Therefore, Abu Bakr, the first caliph of Rasul-Allah ﷺ, was saying, "O people, you must know that if anyone takes away or does not give the rights of a weak one, we are going to support that weak one and he is going to be the most powerful one among the community. And whoever claims that he is a powerful one, he is a rich one, and wants to go and take away the rights of weak ones, he must know that he is weakest one among the community."

---

[14]Nation, community, faith community. An important point is being emphasized throughout these paragraphs. First, all people generally must be respected as souls created by Allah and among the most honoured of His creations. At the same time, Muslims are commanded to give appropriate respect to those in authority, to people of knowledge and erudition, to those whose characters and actions deserve special respect, and to the elders of the community.

Where is Islam? Finished! Where is humanity? Just by name; finished! Yes. Therefore, I am asking forgiveness that I am putting my feet towards you. I must keep respect for you, but for certain reasons I am putting my feet like this.

That is the essence of Islam. And in Islam, mankind are most valued in the Divine Presence because of their obedience. According to your obedience and good manners, Allah Almighty will give you more honour here and Hereafter.

Islam does not make a difference among people except what we said—according to their dealings with people and dealings with their Lord. And Islam orders people to try to give their most high respect to Allah and to do their best for His servants.

Two rules only: you must try to give your most high respect to your Lord, Allah Almighty, and to be most kind and do your best for His servants, for His creatures. That is Islam. Whoever harms people, he is not from Islam.

Eh, saying, "That is an African person, that is an Asian person, that is a European one." Western people, they think that they are first class mankind because their color is white. If of a different color, they are going to be of no value. No! Not by color but by your actions, your dealings, your respect to Allah Almighty, and respect to Allah Almighty passes through respecting His servants.

Keep respect for everyone! Then respect will come to you, also; everything giving you respect. Give respect to everything and everything will give respect to you.

May Allah forgive us and bless you. For the honour of the most honoured one in His Divine Presence, Sayyidina. Muhammad ﷺ—*Fateha!* ▲

7

Heavenly Patronage, Satanic Patronage"

A'udhu bil-Lahi min ash-Shaytani-r-rajeem. Bismillahi-r-Rahmani-r-Raheem. La hawla wa la quwwata illa bil-Lahi-l-'Aliyi-l-'Azheem.

We are asking from our Patrons.[1] And when we say "Patrons," it is those who are able to control their egos.

'Patron' is a title among people. If a person is the director of company or a business, people may say, "This is our patron." That is a patron in common people's understanding. A patron is in control of his business and those who are working for him in a company. Everything is under his control.

A real Patron, in the Divine Presence, is that person who can control his ego. That is a real Patron. Therefore, when They[2] said to me, "Patrons," I was surprised. Who is a patron, and patronage is for whom?

---

[1][Tr.] *velinimet*, benefactor.
[2]See footnote 2.

All *awliya* have patronage because a person can't be a saint without being able to control himself, to control his ego. If a person is able to control his ego, then a heavenly patronage is going to be given to him. But that person is not going to be a patron quickly. Allah Almighty is saying, *"Wa la-nabluannakum,*[3] I am going to try you. Without trying you, I will not accept you."

When you can be successful under divine trials, then you should be given that title. "That person, that servant, you may trust in him." It goes to the Prophet ﷺ.[4] "That servant, you can trust in him. Use him for your *ummah*, for your nation."

No one gives responsibility in a war to a private, no. Responsibility is given to a lieutenant or captain or major because they can be trusted, not giving it to a person from the rank-and-file army. No, can't be. And those Patrons who have been checked, the Prophet ﷺ may trust in them and give their tasks to them, how they should act for saving his ummah, his nation, from the assaults of Shaytan and devils, giving that power to them because they are trustworthy persons. And a person can't be trustworthy if he isn't able to control his ego, no.

Therefore, Patrons, who are *awliya*, have been appointed by the Seal of the Prophets ﷺ to look after his *ummah* so

---

[3] *"And We will surely test you."* (2:155)

[4] That is, *awliya* observe how a candidate for patronage handles the tests he/she is sent. When the tests are successfully passed and that servant is cleared by *awliya* in the spiritual world, the matter goes to the Prophet ﷺ, who is continuously looking after the affairs of his *ummah* from the spiritual sphere. The Prophet ﷺ then confers on that servant the rank of Patron, i.e., *veli/wali*, saint, or *velinimet*, benefactor.

that people will not to be harmed by Shaytan and Shaytan's groups or devils, so they will not deal in evil. Everyone, if not reaching a Patron for training under his command, may easily fall into the hands of satanic groups and devils, and should be employed for evil.

And people are in two groups, one employed under the patronage of Patrons to do their best for their Lord, to be good servants to their Lord, and also to do their best for their Lord's creation, for their Lord's servants. That group of people who accept that training under the patronage of Patrons, of *awliya*, they are fortunate ones. But if they do not accept, they will fall into the hands of devils.

All the prophets were the best ones for their nations. They were sent to people to save them from falling into the hands of devils. But most people ran away from those patrons of mankind—and the first level Patrons are prophets. When prophets came to their nations, most people ran away from them and became enemies, going against them.

Throughout all the historical periods of mankind, beginning with Adam, the Lord of Heavens sent thousands and thousands of Patrons, heavenly Patrons, to call people to their Lord and to call them to eternity. But they ran away, because Satan and shaytanic groups also have patronage from shaytanic headquarters, and satanic headquarters takes that patronage from Satan. People preferred to run after them and they refused the best way of life. And they denied anything after this temporary life and said, "No life after this life," denying eternity, denying eternal life.

What happened after that? The Lord of Heavens sent His divine anger upon them, and when the divine anger came, it took them away. *Qur'an al-Kareem*⁵ mentions what happened to those nations that refused the patronage of Heavens and ran after the patronage of shaytanic people. They lost everything and reached a bad end.

And we are saying "patronage" for the last and most honoured prophet, Sayyidina Muhammad ﷺ. He called people to eternity; he called people to an honourable life here and to eternal life for eternity in the Divine Presence. Mostly people ran away and they fought him. He called them to Paradise and they wanted to kill him.

What happened to those who were against Sayyidina Muhammad's heavenly patronage? The heads of that shaytanic patronage, its 'chairmen,' were killed and thrown, one by one, on top of each other into a well in the desert, and they finished and vanished. And the final victory belonged to the Seal of Prophets ﷺ, and those who accepted his patronage and controlled their egos went not down but up to Heavens.

Now you can find some of those selected, chosen people who accepted the Seal of the Prophets and his patronage.⁶ Anywhere they are buried, you may find their graves like a Paradise-place, people giving them their high respect. Because they said "Yes" to the heavenly invitation, Allah honoured them. And Muslims are keeping respect for them up to today, visiting them, and when you visit their holy places, you find a satisfaction, contentment and peace when you go into their holy presence.

---

⁵The Noble Qur'an.

⁶That is, his *Sahabah*, Companions, from the first generation of Muslims.

Their presence is holy. But some square-headed people are claiming and saying that when Muslims visit the tombs of *Sahabah*, they are worshipping them.

No! We know that their presence is a holy presence. We are not saying their presence is a divine presence; no, we can't say that. But we are keeping the order of Allah Almighty that says, *"Wa la tansau-l-fadla bainakum."*[7] Allah Almighty is reminding believers and ordering them not to forget those who did their best for their Lord. Their Lord's representatives, *Sahabah*, you must keep respect for them. That is an order.

I am sorry to say that they are Arabs but they never understand the Holy Qur'an.[8] *"Wa la tansaw-l-fadla baynakum." Sahabah* are *ahlu-l-fadl.*[9] They have *radi-Allahu 'anhum wa radu 'anhu.*[10] Allah Almighty is granting them His divine pleasure; He respects them. Then how are you *not* going to respect them? But they are destroying their tombs over them and making their graves not to be known, even not to write their names on them! *Allahumma, la haula wa la quwwata illa bil-Lahi-l-'Aliyi-l-'Azheem!*[11]

---

[7]*"And do not forget precedence* [fadl] *among yourselves."* (2:237)

[8]Referring to the current Wahhabis who are propagating such inaccurate and superficial understandings of Islam.

[9]People of precedence.

[10]*"Allah is pleased with them and they are pleased with Him."* (9;100, 58:22, 98:8)

[11]O our Lord, there is no power or might except with Allah, the Most High, the Almighty.

Most of you have gone to Istanbul, also, on your way, so many people. There is Abu Ayyub al-Ansari[12] ⚔, Allah bless him. When you go and visit him, your feeling changes. Then you smell such a beautiful scent, and when you look, you feel *khashiyat*,[13] such a sweet fear in your heart, and you would like to be with him [Abu Ayyub] always. Where are Abu Jahl[14] and others who rejected heavenly patronage through Sayyidina Muhammad ﷺ?

And now, no *haya*.[15] Some Arabs are asking to take away the Prophet's name, to write only *"La ilaha illa-Llah"* and not to put *"Muhammadun Rasul-Allah"*[16] after it. And they are building mosques, not writing the name of Sayyidina Muhammad ﷺ, writing only *"Allah Allah Allah."* But Allah does not accept that from servants if they do not accept Sayyidina Muhammad ﷺ, because He says, *"Wa kaffa bil-Lahi shahidan: Muhammadun Rasul-Allah"*[17] Who has been given such an honour? Allah Almighty is saying, "I am witnessing that he is My prophet. I am putting his name after My Name."

---

[12] A Companion of the Prophet, who was martyred in Istanbul at the age of ninety in a battle between the Muslims and the Romans in the year 669 or 678 C.E.. He is buried in the European side of the city at the Eyyüp Sultan Mosque.

[13] Reverential fear, awe, reverence, respect.

[14] The Prophet's uncle and his cohorts, the vicious enemies of the Prophet and Islam, who were killed in a battle with the Muslims and put in a dried-up well.

[15] Shame, modesty.

[16] "Muhammad is the Messenger of Allah, may Allah's blessings and peace be on him."

[17] *"And Allah is Sufficient as witness. Muhammad is the messenger of Allah."* (48:28-29)

So many places I am going and looking for the inscription, *"La ilaha illa-Llah, Muhammadun Rasul-Allah."*[18] I am saying, "Where is *'La ilaha illa-Llah, Muhammadun Rasul-Allah'*? Is this is a depot, a warehouse, or it is a place of prayer? Why are you not mentioning your faith, that no one can be Muslim without saying, *'La ilaha illa-Llah, Muhammadun Rasul-Allah?'* How are you doing this?"

Those who are accepting, they are on the respected level, respected by their Lord and respected by all Muslims. Others have just left. Therefore, now people they are in need of heavenly patronage because they are running after the satanic patronage. The patron of this world now, among all nations, is Shaytan, and people are accepting, through democracy, the satanic patronage. We do not accept democracy. We accept what Allah sent,[19] and He sent *malik*, king, and *sultan*.

They changed it because the satanic patronage ordered them to take away kings and *sultans*, and they are falling into endless troubles and sufferings now. But for every period there is a limit. Their limit is going to finish; one year, less or more, and there must come heavenly patronage here, now. Arabs, you must understand first! Arabs have left. *Iman*, faith, came from them first and went away from their end first.

---

[18]"There is no deity except Allah, Muhammad is the Messenger of Allah," the Islamic Declaration of Faith *(Shahadah)*.

[19]Through divine revelation in the Old and New Testaments and the Holy Qur'an.

May Allah forgive me and give me power to take away all shaytanic patronage. I am the weakest one, but it is enough to clean that patronage, shaytanic patronage. Even if I am the weakest one, I can do it. For cleaning the W.C., no need to call the *sultan*, "Come and clean." No, I can do this. I am asking, "Give the order. I will clean, from East to West." Without that order, I am nothing; with that order, I am everything I have less than the power of an ant but if the order comes, it is enough to clean. One person may clean—clean ten worlds, also, not only one.

May Allah forgive me! For the most honoured one in His Divine Presence—*Fateha!* ▲

8

THE FALLACY OF "ECONOMIC CRISIS" CAUSING THE PEOPLE MISERY

A'udhu bil-Lahi min ash-Shaytani-r-rajeem. Bismillahi-r-Rahmani-r-Raheem. La hawla wa la quwwata illa bil-Lahi-l-'Aliyi-l-'Azheem.

Masha'Allah,[1] everyone here is a first-class clever ones! Everyone, first-class professors, are coming to me. Say something. I may learn. If I speak, no one learns.

We are happy, we are fortunate. We must say that no one can be, never can be, like us. Why?

The Lord of Heavens is giving us permission to say His Holy Name, *"Al-laah!"* Say, *"Al-laah Al-laah Al-laah! Subhanallah, subhanallah, subhanallah! La ilaha illa-Llah, Muhammadun Rasul-Allah, 'alaihi-s-salat Allah wa salamuhu!*[2]-

---

[1] As Allah willed.
[2] "Glory be to Allah (three times). There is no deity except Allah. Muhammad is the Messenger of Allah, Allah's blessings and peace be upon him."

A'udhu bil-Lahi min ash-Shaytani-r-rajeem. Bismillahi-r-Rahmani-r-Raheem. La haula wa la quwwata illa bil-Lahi-l-'Aliyi-l-'Azheem.

Shaytan is very angry with you. Allah is happy, Shaytan unhappy. Try every time to make Satan unhappy, try every moment to make your Lord happy with you.

Two ways only, no another way. Two ways, like a magnet; two poles, positive, negative. This side is positive, to be with Allah; that side is negative, to be with Shaytan. Every, every action that we do either takes us to this side, making Allah happy, or carries us to Shaytan's side, to be unhappy.

I am asking people, "O people, what do you think about the inhabitants, the people now living on earth—perhaps they are six billion or reaching seven billion? Are they making their Lord happy or making Shaytan happy?"

Your answer must be to say that the people living on earth, ninety-nine per cent of them, are making Shaytan happy, not trying to make Allah Almighty happy with them. You think that Bangladeshi people are happy people now? You think that Arabs are happy people now? Can you think that Russians are happy people now? Do you think that Turks are happy people now? No, because they are not trying to make their Lord happy, and it is written for them not to be happy, to be *un*happy.

[Parodies:] "Economic crisis!"[3] It is the biggest lie, biggest lie, that they are saying this. It is not an economic cri-

---

[3]This talk was given in early 2004.

sis—no! That is a shaytanic teaching to cover up the important points that are making people unhappy, saying, "Because of the economic crisis people are unhappy." The biggest liar and most cursed one is Shaytan and those who are following Shaytan! No. They have enough money, more than enough money. They are *iddikhir*, saving, saving billions and trillions. Why would they not be happy?

Eh, ya Rabbi, ya Allah, Allah! Ar-Rahman 'allam al-Qur'an—Allah, Allah—khalaq al-insan, 'allamu al-bayan. Allahu Akbar! Ar-Rahman,[4] He is Almighty Allah, proclaiming His endless Mercy Oceans.

"O people, I am covering with you with My blessings, with My Mercy Oceans. But you are drunk, not understanding, running away from Me, and I am that One whose blessings reach from *thara* to *sidrat al-muntaha*.[5] I am that One, your Lord, the Lord of all creation. You can't find any unit of creation—you may say an atom or less than an atom—without My blessings or without being surrounded by My blessings.

"My blessings are given to you for being in existence and My blessings are running after you to reach you, but you are escaping, O foolish ones. And I am giving you minds to think, but you are not thinking; giving you intellect for balancing everything, but you are not using your

---

[4]Eh, O my Lord, O Allah, Allah. *"The Most Merciful taught the Qu'ran"*—Allah, Allah—*"created the human being [and] taught him exposition"* [55:1-4]. Allah is Most Great! The Most Merciful, He is Almighty Allah . . .

[5]*Thara*: soil, earth; *Sidrat al-Muntaha*: the Tree in the seventh (i.e., highest) Heaven beyond which no human or angel has ever passed besides the Holy Prophet during his *Me'raj* (Ascension) to the Divine Presence.

intellect and falling into troubles, and you are running into Hells. I am preventing you, but you are running to them."

Wrong direction! The wrong direction brings every trouble. Those who do not keeping warnings from Heavens *must* fall into troubles, no doubt. That is the real reason, not, as Shaytan and his representatives are claiming, that the crisis on earth is the result of economic aspects. They are liars!

I heard today in that Shaytan's box, TV, that the richest one among Turkish people just passed away in the morning—Sabancı, they were saying.

He was a boy from a poor family, but he was such an active person, and he was trying and working, working, and making a good business, and they were saying that he was the richest one in Turkey. He passed away, *subhanallah*. Yesterday he became ill; in intensive care for one day only (some people, for weeks or months, even years, are in such a situation). That person was doing charity, also, and *subhanallah*, only lying down for one day and the second morning, finished.

That one, I never saw him when he was happy. Always he was sad, always he was unhappy, perhaps not for himself but for his people that he was living with, their situations giving him sadness, and he was the richest one but unhappy. He was unhappy and passed away unhappy; his richness never giving him happiness, no; he was sad and passed away in such a way. His Creator, the Lord of the Heavens, Allah Almighty, He knows about him, and He is dealing with that servant as He likes.

I mean to say, don't think that happiness is with material aspects; no. He was a billionaire, not with Turkish money [laughter]—a billionaire of dollars, green, green paper. And he always lived sad and he passed away sad.

Therefore, I mean to say that what Shaytan is saying to people about the crisis and sufferings that they are in—that it is only for economic reasons because everyone's salaries are coming down and so many businesses are shut down— no! I am saying, as an example, that that person was sad although he had a billion dollars and big areas for factories, everything. He had a gallery of antique pieces, perhaps ten million or more dollars, but he was sad, he was unhappy.

Shaytan is teaching people that your sadness is because you don't have money. And I am saying to Shaytan, "What about *that* person? Why are you lying to people, why are you trying to deceive people? That was such a person."

And before that one, a very rich person, richer than him—they are saying the Datsun or Nissan or such a factory owner in Japan, whose wealth may have reached a hundred times more than Sabancı, the Turkish one—he was unhappy, and unhappiness made him open the balcony of the highest floor of his apartment building and throw himself down.

You heard about it? What was the name of this factory? No Japanese people here? [Suggestion: Korea.] What was his factory ? Hyundai, the famous.

[Someone else tells about an American tycoon who killed himself.] *Shuf*, look! Bringing another example. Spitting on Shaytan [laughter], cheating people and saying that money gives happiness. Therefore, spitting again! Once again, spitting on Shaytan, cheating people!

Look, he is such a liar, *ghashash,* cheat! The biggest cheat is Shaytan, and people are running after him. They are saying "Yes, for economic reasons we are unhappy," and I am showing them such people. And ____ is saying, also, that one of the biggest businessmen shot himself.

Allah, Allah! Ya Rabbi, ya Allah![6] We are asking for forgiveness. Keep our minds, keep our faith, O our Lord, not to lose our minds and do something against ourselves When a person loses his intellect and his mind, he does useless things and harms himself and harms others—and harms creation, also. Whoever does harm, whoever does unsuitable things, he harms, gives trouble, to everything in existence.

Beware of Satan! Guard yourself! It is something else that is making people unhappy. Those who are worshipping *dunya,* they are unhappy. Whoever is worshipping Allah, they are happy ones.

May Allah forgive us and bless you! For the honour of the most honoured one in His Divine Presence, Sayyidina Muhammad—*Fateha!* ▲

---

[6] "O my Lord, O Allah."

9

IN YESTERDAY, OUT TOMORROW

A'udhu bil-Lahi min ash-Shaytani-r-rajeem. Bismillahi-r-Rahmani-r-Raheem. La hawla wa la quwwata illa bil-Lahi-l-'Aliyi-l-'Azheem.

Sayyidina Nuh, Noah, Allah bless him, reached the oldest age. Perhaps no one except him lived one thousand years. It was a long life, perhaps the longest life among prophets. And the people who were with Nuh ﷺ when he was leaving this life and going on, were asking, "How did you find this life? What do you think? What is your *intibah*, your observation? What is your view? You are surely more than one thousand years old. What are your thoughts about your long life? Tell!"

And he was saying, "I am now just in the position of a person, who, during his travels, reaches a inn, a *karavansaray*.[1] I see that yesterday I came in and today I am going out. Even though I was here one thousand years and more,

---

[1] Here, Sheikh Nazim adds parenthetically: "Old-time people were resting at rest houses or guest houses. Now, at so many places, big buildings, government buildings, there are signs, "IN ➡ —OUT ➡," that *ok*, arrow, showing "IN ➡ —OUT ➡."

now finally I am like such a person coming to an inn, going in and finishing his job and getting out."

Allah Almighty is saying, *"Faqsusi-l-qasasa la'allhum yatafakarun."*[2] He is ordering His prophets, and particularly the Seal of the Prophets, the last one, to tell the stories of nations, and also what happened to them and what is going to happen like a story, because everything that happened yesterday is written as a story. We have left it behind.

So many days, weeks, months, years, even centuries, have passed. Where are they? Anything you have kept from that time has only become like a story, a tale. Perhaps you may say, and living people may say, "You are telling fairy tales. You can't bring any evidence about the lives of so many nations."

What happened, it is only in our imagination. We may imagine, we may read about their lives, but it is only what we *think* about their lives, trying to make it up in our imagination. Everything that happened, everything past, so many countless actions, countless events, countless happenings, just took place and passed away, with nothing to touch them now. And that heavenly order to the Seal of the Prophets[3] is an order to everyone, also, to read or to hear what happened in past days, the passing centuries of mankind.

For what? Allah is making clear the purpose of that order: to think about it, what happened of goodness; what

---

[2]*"So narrate the stories [of prophets in the Qur'an], that perhaps they may reflect."* (7:176)

[3]The order addressed to the Prophet in 7:176 cited above to narrate the stories of prophets..

happened of badness; what happened to nations or to kings, to *sultans*, to emperors, to *padishahs*,[4] to high level people or first level people, because people are not on the same level, no.

It is a wrong idea to see people on the same level. No; that is a wrong idea that socialism brought, saying "No difference." But do you look the same as him? Does he look the same as that one? No! How you are saying that everyone is on the same level?

Do you think that Allah Almighty produces as factories produce, everything the same model? No! Those foolish people think that Allah Almighty gives everyone the same size, the same outward appearance and the same inner life. No! That is foolishness and that is from satanic teachings, Shaytan claiming that mankind, all of them, are the same — the same, no difference among them. That is the biggest wrong. How? Do you think that He has a man factory, men getting out from this side, women from that side?

Therefore, sometimes I get angry with some girls. If someone asks them for marriage, they bring so many qualifications, saying [parodies], "I would like my husband not to be too *kısa*, short. I don't like him, also, to be three meters tall, like Americans." (Any American here? No.) "And I don't like my husband to be so fat. I don't like his mouth to be up to his ears. I don't like my husband's ears to be like elephants' ears." [Laughter.]

Important points, these, very important, for marriage! Eh! If young ones ask [parodies], "I am interested that my wife should be like a stick." [Laughter.]

---

[4]Ruler, king, sultan.

"Take two sticks, do like this and rest. Take!"

"I don't like my wife to be more than forty kilograms because if I need to carry her, I can put her on my shoulder . . ." [Laughter.]

And I am saying, "Up to today, I never found an *ilân*, advertisment, that says, 'O people, the twenty-first century's technicians, technologists, are building a made-to-order factory for girls." And I have never heard that anyone has built a factory for foolish young ones who make a description of a wife and give it to them, and then what he likes comes out—their colors, their height, their eyes.

"I don't like her eyes. Very small."

"Eh! Take and put another eye."

What are we saying? We are saying that Allah Almighty gives everyone a speciality. From the beginning up to the end, perhaps *ummata Muhammad*, the nation of Muhammad, may reach 124 billion. If you do not believe me, add them, count them. You have so many computers. Ask a computer, "What do you think about Shaykh's words, what he is claiming about the number of Muslims?" What does the answer come to, what does that computer's shaytan say?

Saying, "All computers are under the control of shaytans, to make your heads another head, a satanic head."

Eh! I am saying, "What are you doing?"

"I am touching this."

"What is happening?"

"There is a mouse running on this screen."

"Bring my eyeglasses to look. Very small. Is there a mouse of such a size?"

"Yes, and it is running, going, coming, and giving news to me."

And I am saying, "You are taking news from a mouse, not taking it from Heavens? What is your honor, following a mouse, not following heavenly orders? *La haula wa la quwwata . . . !*"

Everyone has a special destiny. You can't find two persons with the same destiny, *muqaddarat*,[5] their private life lines that they must be on. They can't get out from that. *"Wa kullun fi falaqin yasbahun,"*[6] each one has a special orbit. Everyone must move on his orbit, can't be outside it.

Therefore, you may find your position when you hear what happened to men in past times, and you may take a lesson that may correct your steps—who was walking in a correct direction and what happened to them, and who was walking on the wrong way and what happened to them; to learn something; to use your minds and to reach safety. You may choose the Safe Way.

I was in London, and I saw, written on a big building, "Safeway." I asked, "Oh, Safeway! I am trying to show people the Safe Way. I must go in to ask what is their Safe Way."

---

[5]Decreed, preordained.
[6]*"And each one is swimming in an orbit."* (36:40)

I entered and asked, but they said, "No, O Shaykh. This is a big market."

"What is written there?"

"Safeway."

People, not to be cheated, must come to the Safe Way. Safe Way, the real Safe Way, is the way of Heavens, and the dangerous, un-safe way, it is the way of shaytans and devils.

Now people are running on the wrong way, with wrong steps, and every time they are touching a dangerous happening and they are suffering. Yes. Through historical periods, through traditional knowledge, we are looking and seeing. And what Noah ﷺ said is true.

Maybe if Noah ﷺ, instead of living one thousand years, had lived 100,000 years, his statement would finally have been as he said before, at the time when he lived 1000 years. Maybe if he had lived for one million years, he would finally have said, "I just entered from the "IN" direction and now I am going from the "OUT" direction." Even if it was billions, trillions, quadrillions of years, you would finally say, "Just yesterday I entered and today I am going out."

O people, the most dangerous thing for mankind which is making them fall into bottomless troubles and unsolved problems, is to think that they are living a never-ending life. And they are cheating themselves, you are cheating yourself. Therefore, those who are ignorant of heavenly teachings are always falling into troubles and problems and miseries, here and Hereafter.

The fortunate one or clever one, or those whose hearts are opened with divine lights, are looking and seeing. They are looking as a person taking a train always looks when the train stops, looking at the writing of the name of the station because he knows his station and he is waiting. He does not sleep; he is awake not to pass it, looking. And man must look each day and see if this is my station where I am going to disembark, where I will get down—looking, because one day he *must* get down, we *must* get down.

We will not always go with that train, no. Wherever is written on our ticket, we must get down. We must prepare ourselves for our heavenly journey. The earthly journey is going to finish, ending, and the heavenly journey will begin. If you do not take care about your heavenly journey, you should be thrown there, and you may lose your chance to reach to your heavenly station in the Divine Presence.

May Allah forgive us and grant us, through His divine representatives, to reach people who are now living on earth but do not know anything about their heavenly stations, to save people and guide them to their divine stations in the Heavens. For the honour of the most honoured one in His Divine Presence, Sayyidina. Muhammad ﷺ—*Fateha!* ▲

1o

THE HIGH HONOR OF ADDRESSING OUR LORD BY HIS HOLY NAME "ALLAH"

A'udhu bil-Lahi min ash-Shaytani-r-rajeem. Bismillahi-r-Rahmani-r-Raheem. La hawla wa la quwwata illa bil-Lahi-l-'Aliyi-l-'Azheem.

Through *"Bism-illahi-r-Rahmani-r-Rahim,"* He, Almighty, is giving "Allah," His greatest Name that includes all His Holy Names in itself. When we say "Allah," we are making *dhikr* with all His Holy Names.

"Allah" is the most renowned Name on earth and in Heavens. But His Holy Name is now used only among Muslims, and people of other nations and other religions are not saying it, they are not mentioning that His name is "Allah".

English people, what do they say? "God." French, what do they say? *"Dieu."* Greeks, what do they say? *"Theos."* *'Ajam,*[1] what do they say? *"Khoda;"* Farsi. Germans, what do they say? *"Gott."* Italians? *"Deo."* None of them is

---

[1] Iranis.

His Holy Name. Allah never accepts "God, *Theos, Deo, Khoda, Gott"*—no.

The Arabic language is a big ocean. We are not saying an endless ocean, but the biggest ocean among languages is Arabic. The *mufradat*, terms, that other languages use can't give the meanings that a single word can give in Arabic. You may say *"Subhan Allah,"* but you can't find any religion, any language, that can bring the meaning of *"subhan"* in a single word, no. And there are hundreds and thousands of examples. Therefore, Allah Almighty used the Arabic language for the Holy Qur'an, the most important heavenly Message.

And in the Arabic language there is *"ilah,"* god,[2] and *"'uluhiya,"* to be god.[3] *"Ilah"* is a common noun, not a proper noun. "God" is only *muradif*,[4] a meaning similar to the words *"ilah, Gott, Theos, Deo, Khoda,"* and *"Tanrı"* in Turkish.

"Ilah" is a common noun but "Allah" is *isim khass*, a proper noun. *"Tanrı"* in Turkish—that is a common noun, not a proper noun; no. And you can't find in any other language a proper noun about which Allah Almighty says, "I am that One." He does not accept to be addressed as, "O my God"; no.

"I am your Lord. My name is Allah. My name is not 'God'. 'God' is a word for understanding that servanthood is the *sifa*, characteristic, of servants. Lordship is for Me—Lordship, *'uluhiya*. And My name is Allah," He is saying. It is His proper Name, His proper noun, for everyone that is

---

[2]Deity.
[3]Divinity, Lordship, Godhood.
[4]Equivalent, corresponding in meaning.

living on earth and for heavenly beings. They are saying, *"Ya Huwa, ya Allah!"*⁵

Therefore, people are not reaching honour when they do not address the Lord of Heavens as "O Allah." "O my God"—no! I am saying that it is impossible to bring a word that is similar to His well-known Name, "Allah"—"Allah" to every creature on earth, in Heavens. And He is looking for His servant to say, *"Ya Allah,"* not to say, "O my God!"

"What is this? My name is not 'God.' My name is 'Allah.'"

English people, for every occasion, are saying, "O my God!" Whom are you addressing? Who is that, your god? Without a name, your god? Oh-oh! Do you think that saying "O my son" or "O my donkey" is enough? What is this?

"What do you mean? No name for Me? You even give a name to your horse!" Say, "His Name is *Allah!*" Why, why are you not saying His proper Name? *Allahu Akbar!* Can you translate *"Allahu Akbar"* into your language?"

[A German *murid* suggests, *"Allah ist ein grössen,"* and ends by saying, "It is impossible. It doesn't say anything." Shaykh laughs.]

"Who is that one?"

"A man."

"No name?"

"No. Only 'a man.'"

"What is his name? Who is that?"

---

⁵"O He [who is Allah], O Allah!"

"**A man!**"

"'A man'. No name?"

Saying, "God." Without a name, God? Therefore, everyone who does not reach that level, his level is the lowest level, the lowest level.[6]

We are trying to know Him, and if you are want to know someone, first you ask his name. "His name is His Majesty King George the Fifth." Then, when you go into his majestic presence, you may address to him as, "O Your Majesty, King of England and Emperor of India, King George the Fifth." And when you come to address Allah Almighty, don't say, "O my God," because the word "god" [*ilah*] may be singular and may be plural, also. Plural, "gods". They may say "gods," their gods, but there is no plural for "Allah". For everything you may find a plural except for His Holy Name, "Allah".

And people are *mahrum*, deprived. They have lost the chance throughout their lives to say His holy Name, "Allah". Millions of people go away from this life like this, not saying "Allah."

For what reason? "Because Muslims say 'Allah,' we must not say 'Allah.'" But if you do not say His Holy

---

[6]That is, the Creator is not an abstraction, a concept, or a thing. Rather, He is the Divine Being whose Holy Name is above all other names. "Allah" is the unique, sacred Name by which He refers to Himself in verse after verse of the Qur'an, informing mankind of His identity so that we may have the privilege of addressing Him by that sacred Name which belongs uniquely to Him. .

Name, He does not accept your addressing Him as "O my God," saying, "Go and look for your god."

On the Day of Resurrection, people will come with their idols and with the names that the nations that lived in past times used for their idols. For example, the Greek people believed in polytheism, and the head god, chief god, was Zeus. "Zeus" then came to be "Theos". Now, Greek people use "Theos," and the name Theos comes from Zeus, the chief of their gods during the time before Christ.

They had so many. Therefore, on the Day of Resurrection everyone will bring their gods with them, in front of them, inscribed "Our god". Only Muslims will say "Allah". Allah Almighty will send each group of people with their gods—and also, they have goddess. *Allahu Akbar*, there are goddesses, also!

Do you also have "goddess" in your language? Must be; *tanrı*, god, *tanrıça*, goddess. Yes. Venus or Aphrodite, they are goddesses. They have gods and also goddesses; they have plurals and they have female goddesses, male gods. Still they use that, still they have not come to proclaim that the Name of the Lord of Heavens is "Allah," no plural, no similar for Him.

Their heads are like rocks! They have reached the twenty-first century but they are not looking at such a reality. Still they are using their imagination, throughout thousands of years. How should they reach peace? Their gods or their goddess will give them peace, they think.[7]

Yesterday I was at the monastery. They were showing me icons; they are not getting away from icons. They are still underground, the lowest, lowest level. They think that icons give them something, running after them.

Yes; imagination! From East to West, from North to South, until mankind is going to say "Allah," no way for them to be saved, here and Hereafter. You understand? His Name, our Lord's Name, is "Allah." *Ya Allah, ya Allah!. An-ta Allah, Huwa Allah. Allahu, Allahu. Hasbun Allah wa ni'am al-wakil.*[8]

Kafa bina sharafan.[9] It is more than enough, that honour of saying "Allah"! To Europeans, Americans, who say that we are at the top point of honour because we are Western people, I am saying, "You are at the lowest point because you do not say, *"Ya Allah!"* That honour is enough. To say "Allah" gives honour to us. We are such fortunate people that we have been honoured to say and to address our Lord, *"Ya Allah, ya Allah, ya Allah!."*

May Allah forgive us! For the honour of the Seal of the Prophets, the most honoured one in His Divine Presence, *Rasul-Allah* ﷺ — *Fateha!* ▲

---

[7]In a modern context, this refers to icons, statues, paintings and other graphic objects of veneration in various faiths.
[8] O Allah, O Allah! You are Allah, He is Allah. Allah, He; Allah, He. Allah suffices for us, and how excellent a Protector.
[9]It is sufficient honour for us.

11

THE POWER OF WORKING FOR ALLAH

A'udhu bil-Lahi min ash-Shaytani-r-rajeem. Bismillahi-r-Rahmani-r-Raheem. La hawla wa la quwwata illa bil-Lahi-l-'Aliyi-l-'Azheem.

The best work for people, what is that? To work for Allah is the best work. You know another work, another patron or boss, who pays you?

Once there was a person, and everything he had was finished. Nothing remained at his home to eat. His family was hungry and there was nothing to eat, and he wanted to go and work. And at that time, most people were workers or laborers.

He took his axe and shovel, and went to the market, sitting and waiting for someone to call him, "Come and work for me." The workers were sitting there. If anyone came for them, they went. If not, they went home without anything.

That person went and sat, waiting, waiting from morning up to midday before *Dhuhr*[1]. Most people looked for workers early in the morning, and no one asked him. And he said, "Today, no one is asking me to work for him. I can work for my Lord. I am going to the mosque."

Making *wudu*[2] and entering, sitting, praying, reciting Holy Qur'an, making *tasabih*[3] up to evening. Then in the evening, he went home. And his wife asked, "O my husband, did you bring something? Did you work today?"

And he said, "Yes, I worked today."

"What you bring?"

And he said, "My employer said, 'Not today. Tomorrow I am going to pay you.' We can be patient today, we can drink water."

And the second day, he was early, taking his tools, going to the same workers' market, sitting there, looking. No one asked, "Come and work for me." And he said, "Today, also, if no one employs me, I must go to my Lord's work. I can work for Him."

Making *wudu*, sitting, up to evening. When he came home in the evening, his wife asked, "O my husband, O my man, did you work today and did you bring something?"

"Yes, I worked, I worked."

"What did you bring?"

---

[1] The second of the five daily prayers, observed from noon to mid-afternoon.

[2] The prescribed ablution or washing for prayers.

[3] Phrases of glorification of God, *dhikr*.

"He promised me tomorrow, not today. You must be patient. What can we do?" They drank water and slept. And people have everything but they do not thank Allah!

They slept. The third day, earlier in the morning, he went to the same place for workers, sitting. People came, taking others to work but leaving him. And he said, "I shall work today."

He went to the mosque, making *wudu* and praying. When it was evening, he was so sorry that for three days he had brought nothing, and he went out. And he took out his *mandil*, handkerchief, and he took sand, very fine sand, from the floor of the mosque, putting it and saying, "I can go, taking this. If she asks, I can say, 'I have brought *daqiq*, flour.'"

He took it and went home and knocked at the door, and slowly he put that handkerchief full of sand behind the door. And his wife came to the door, so happy, so happy, and there was a good smell of food, everything, and his wife hugged him.

"What happened?"

"O my husband, you worked three days for such a rich one! And he sent us a covered copper plate, and his servant gave it to me and said, 'This is the *yaumiya*, salary, for two days, and this is three days' salary. My boss is sending it to you. Take it. That is his three days' salary.'"

"I opened it and it was full of gold! I took only one piece and went to market, and with one gold piece I loaded a donkey. I brought everything, I can do everything now. O my husband, your boss is such a blessed one, such a rich one! *Subhanallah!*" she said.

He was amazed. And he wanted to take that *mandil*, handkerchief to throw it away, but when he reached for it, it was so heavy. "I brought sand, but now I can't lift it off the ground." And he opened it and all that sand had become gold. And he said, "*Alhamdulillah* that I worked! O-oh-h!"

Whoever works for Him, He is the richest one. No one can be rich; all of us are poor ones, needy from Him. He is the only One that has no needs, needless. Never—He is never in need. Therefore I am asking you, "Which boss can give you, if you work for him, more than the Lord of Heavens? O people, you are such foolish ones!"

And most people, if you ask, "Do you pray?" they say [parodies], "No. No time for me to pray."

"What do you do?"

"I work, I work hard."

"And for your Lord, no time?"

What does your boss give to you? Only what is enough to eat and drink, and to pay money for the rent. Yes. The most honoured work for mankind, what is that? To work for their Lord! But people are so foolish, running away from their Lord and asking for money or whatever they are in need of from others who may be the richest ones. But that one may sleep as the richest one and when morning comes, not even one euro, one dollar. Finished, bankrupt!

People are foolish! In 2004, the twenty-first century's people are not thinking about this point—that we must work, we must be workers only for our Lord. And He is saying, "I am responsible for your provision, for your *rizq*. I do not leave even an ant without provision. And everything that is in existence is glorifying Me."

That means that everyone has a mouth to glorify. If anyone has a mouth to glorify, it needs to eat something to give power to its mouth. Therefore, even bacteria, viruses, all things, are in need of their provision, and provision is appointed for everyone from the Divine Presence, granted to them.[4] And they [non-human creatures] are so trusting. No doubt for them that their Lord will not forget them. No one, no one, can say, "My Lord forgot my provision." Everything, every creature, takes its provisions from its Lord.

What about mankind? What is this, that people are running away from their Lord? Who else can give to them? If He does not send our provisions from Heavens, who can give to us from the earth, because, if provision does not come from Heavens, everything on earth is going to be dry and finish. If no rains come, no life.

Therefore, O people, think about it! Think about it, because it is so important for you, for your life, for your contentment, for you honour, for your future, for your eternal life. Try to take more care of your Lord's service. Work for Him!

People are saying, "If you don't work, you don't live." But they are *kadhdhab,* they are lying.

Allah Almighty mentioned everything in the Holy Qur'an. When the Children of Israel rebelled against their Lord's command, He punished them by imprisoning them

---

[4] *"There is no creature on earth but that its provision is with Allah."* (11:6)

in the desert of Tih, Sinai. For forty years, no rain came, no crops came from the earth, but daily Allah Almighty sent provisions for them—birds and *helou*, sweet.[5] And they never worked. [Maulana corrects himself.] They worked—for what?

When Allah Almighty expressed His anger against them to Sayyidina Musa, Moses, saying, "Your brothers, your tribe, are rebellious against My orders, so I am going to imprison them to that desert," they said, "Ah! If we are going to be in this desert, there is no *tel*, wire, fence, no *khandaq*, trench," to prevent them from getting out; no walls, like *Banu Isra'il*, the State of Israel, is now building, a big wall for Arabs, and Arabs are looking like this, saying, "A-ah!"

They were saying, "Doesn't matter! We can be there. No *bekci*, watchman, is waiting, no soldiers, nor that *dikenli tel*, barbed wire. No; nothing. We are free here. No police, no immigration office here, to go, to come. No, we are free. We don't care. We can escape!"

And on the morning of the first day they said, "Oh, oh! We must not stay here , we must escape. Even though Moses is saying that we have been imprisoned here—no! We must find a way to get out." And they began from the right hand, for example, to escape.

Going, going, going, going, going, and at sunset they came and looked. "Oh, this is the place from which we be-

---

[5]*Manna wa salwa,* manna and quails. *Manna* is a sticky substance that collects on the bushes of the area. It is eaten to this day, in processed form as candy, in some countries of the Middle East such as Iraq.

gan to walk. That means that it was the wrong direction. Tomorrow we shall follow another way."

On the second day, going from that way, going, going, and in the evening coming from that side to the same place. They said, "Tomorrow, we must go like this." Going, going, going; at sunset coming to the same place each day, till all of them had died and were buried in that area, that desert, not one remaining of those who refused the holy command of Allah Almighty. All of them passed away and were buried. Even Moses ﷺ was buried there. And Allah Almighty sent Yusha[6] ﷺ to the new generation that did not carry the responsibility of their fathers, and he took them away from there. They were in safety.

I am saying, "No work for them except to walk, till no one remained of those people. They never sat, but Allah Almighty sent provisions. When they came, they found their supper or breakfast ready and ate, Allah Almighty granting His *'ataf*,[7] favors, to those disobedient servants. Then what if you are taking care of His servanthood? Is He going to lose you or forget you? It is impossible!

Therefore, O people, try to work for your Lord, Almighty Allah, and everything is going to be in the best way. If not, everything is going to be in the worst way. Now people are in the worst situation, and it is impossible to be saved from that bad situation till they come to work for their Lord.

---

[6]The prophet Joshua.

[7]Compassion, kindliness, sympathy, affection

SHAYKH NAZIM ADIL AL-HAQQANI

May Allah forgive me and bless you! For of the honour of the most honoured one in His Divine Presence, Sayyidina Muhammad ﷺ—*Fateha!* ▲

12

CONCERNING SLAVERY TO SATAN AND EGO

A'udhu bil-Lahi min ash-Shaytani-r-rajeem. Bismillahi-r-Rahmani-r-Raheem. La hawla wa la quwwata illa bil-Lahi-l-'Aliyi-l-'Azheem.

People think, everyone thinks, that they are powerful. No one likes to say, "I am a weak servant." They think that servanthood makes a person down, and our egos want to be up, in a high position or the highest position. No one is happy to be Number Two, Number Three, Number Four. Everyone wants to be Number One.

One, the first row, represents One. There can't be another One. If there were two Ones, there would be two; if three Ones, there would be three; if four Ones, there would be four, but at the top, there must be just One. Therefore, everyone is eager for the Number One position to be for himself because he knows that everyone must be under that Number One and no one can be above that One; no. All other numbers under One are going down.

Therefore, man is not happy even to be Number Two. Everyone wants to be Number One, to be the first citizen, president, king or *sultan*. But is impossible to have more than one king; two *sultans* can't be. One must be over all, and that is the most powerful one. No one is above that One, no one. He is only *one*.

But it is a characteristic of our egos that all of them want to be Number One. And people are running after the impossible. Everyone is saying, "I would like to study, I would like to learn." And they are continuing to study from primary school, secondary school, A level, O level,[1] high school, university, continuing.

I am asking, "Not yet enough?'

"No. I want to be a Ph.D."

I am saying, "Did you finish?"

"Yes. I graduated, but now I want a Ph.D."

For what? After graduating from the university, he says, "Now I am going to study for a Master's degree." For what? To have a diploma, a certificate, so that he may show it to people. "I am this one. I am at the top point. I am, I would like to be Number One. Therefore, I studied to be Number One."

That is our ego's characteristic, never happy to be among common people, no. And now, everywhere, that bad characteristic is finding its field and wanting to grow, in that field, to be Number One. And finally, man wants to reach the point that Allah Almighty was telling to the Seal of the Prophets, Sayyidina Muhammad ﷺ, on the Night Jour-

---

[1] According to the British educational system, used in Cyprus and many other parts of the world.

ney, *Lailat al-Me'raj*:² "O Muhammad, if I were to give a chance to My servants such as I gave to Pharaoh, don't think that anyone would *not* be a Pharaoh. Everyone would run to be a Pharaoh!"

Pharaoh said, "I am Number One." And when he reached that point, he began to say, "I am your God because no one is above me, over me—no.³ I am that one, the first one, but now I am moving up, also, and I am saying, 'I am your Lord. Prostrate to me! All of you are my servants, or all of you are my slaves,'" not "servants". Servanthood carries honour but slavery never carries honour.

And Pharaoh made his nation his slaves. He imposed slavery on all of them and said, "I am your highest Lord. Prostrate to me! Prostrate to me so that I may put my foot on your heads, and you may understand that I am your Lord and all of you are under my feet." That is the shaytanic teaching for nations, for mankind who are feeding their egos. When they feed their egos, their egos become bigger, bigger, bigger, and finally they say, "O people, all of you are under my feet!"

And this is the second pharaonic time, all tyrants representing Pharaoh now. As Pharaoh made his nation to be his slaves under his feet, now, in the name of democracy, all tyrants want to make their nations slaves under their feet. As Allah Almighty is saying—and no one can be more true than Allah Almighty—"If I were to make a field for nations,

---

²Referring to the Prophet's well-documented journey by night and ascension to the seven heavens and the Divine Presence, which is commemorated annually by Muslims on the 27th of the month of Rajab.

³A reference to Pharaoh's saying, *"Ana Rabbukum al-'ala. I am your most exalted Lord"* (79:24). See also 43:51-54.

for people, and they planted their egos in that field, each one of them would grow into a Pharaoh."

Now they are in it, lying and cheating and making people prostrate to them because they have tanks, air force, navy and army; forcing people, threatening people, grinding people, killing people till they are obedient to them, under their feet. That is the twenty-first century's civilization, not a positive but a negative civilization, a satanic civilization. No value for mankind in our day, either for men or women. All of them are only on the lowest level, and tyrants are stepping on them and ordering, "You must be under our command, you must be our slaves. What we are asking from you, you must do, or we will step on your heads and grind you under!"

"*Man 'arafa nafsahu, fa-qad 'arafa Rabba.*"[4] That Number One, that real Number One, is the One who creates, and among creation, those who are asking to be Number One are liars. They are the representatives of Shaytan because Shaytan was asking to be Number One. His main goal was to be Number One in creation.

When Allah Almighty created man, Adam, and said, "Prostrate to him," Shaytan was saying, "How? No, I can't do that. *I* must be Number One, not Adam!"[5]

That was the beginning of arguing in the Divine Presence. "Demon, get out!" Allah Almighty said. "Who are

---

[4]"The one who knows himself knows his Lord."
[5]2:34, 38:74-76.

you to speak in front of My Divine Presence, to say that I must be Number One? O angels, kick him down!"[6]

Shaytan was expecting to be Number One, but now he is the lowest one, and everyone goes to the toilet on his head. Understand? Sewage, toilets, all dirtiness is directed at Shaytan's head. "You want to be Number One. Take it! You are Number One now!"

And for everyone, that is the first *tarbiyah*, training, heavenly training. "All of you are My servants. No one can claim to be Number One in My Divine Presence. No! Number Onehood is only for Me. I am the Lord! I am the Creator! You are My servants."

Allah is not saying "slaves," no. *'Ubudiyah* means servanthood; we have been granted honour through divine service. People are running to get service in the government, and they are so proud to be employed in Her Majesty the Queen's service. What about for Allah? But people are finished. No more do they think about what is the honour of being servants in the divine service of the Lord of Heavens.

How are you expecting peace and happiness and pleasure and contentment and blessings on earth? Impossible! The whole world is following Shaytan, and Shaytan is teaching everyone, "Try to be Number One!"

"How? Only you [Shaytan] are Number One. There is going to be only one Number One. Why you are urging us to be Number One, Number One? How can it be?" But our egos have the same kind of shaytanic quality, shaytanic

---

[6] 2:36, 38; 38:77-78.

characteristic. The same characteristic is in everyone; everyone's ego represents Shaytan in everyone. Therefore, Shaytan is urging his representatives to say, "Try to be Number One."

How? How can it be? Therefore, finished now! Must be changed. This period has just reached the last point and they should be changed, they should be taken away. Those who are living for that purpose, that aim that all nations, all people, are running after if their main goal is to be Number One, that means that all of them are going to be taken away. *Must* be taken away, and a new generation will come that is going to proclaim, "We are Your servants. We are not asking anything more than servanthood, O our Lord. That is the height, the final point of honour—to be Your servants, not to be Number One. Number One is to put our egos under our feet.[7] The Number One position is for the Lord of Heavens, for Allah Almighty. We are not asking for that Number Oneship."

That is *shirk, shirkun khafi*,[8] the secret partnership that Wahhabi people are understanding wrongly.[9] If we speak like this, they are saying, *"Shirk!"* never understanding what partnership is. *Shirk* is not about doing like this, doing like that; that is not *shirk*, partnership. Partnership is letting

---

[7]Meaning that the height of honour is to put our unruly lower selves [*nafs* or ego] under our feet.

[8]*Shirk:* ascribing divinity or its attributes (partnership) to someone or something other than Allah;. *shirkun khafi:* secret, hidden *shirk* through desiring and claiming status and authority for one's ego, and becoming its servant.

[9]That is, by Wahhabis' invalid ascriptions of *shirk* to those who follows shaykhs or pray at the graves of *Sahabah* and, *awliya*.

your ego ask to be Number One. That is *shirk*, the real *shirk* that is prevented, forbidden. But they are finished. They are *çürüdü elma*, rotten, spoiled people; finished. All of them are in *shirk!*

And the Prophet was saying, "*Ash-shirku fi ummati akhfa min dabibi-n-naml*"[10] *Ash-shirk* means to want to be Number One, not to be satisfied with being a servant but wanting to reach Lordship. People are not happy now to proclaim their servanthood. Rather, they want to reach Lordship, and Lordship is only for One, no second. Therefore, everyone who wants to be Number One is asking to be a partner to the Lord of Heavens because only He has the right to be Number One, no one else.

May Allah forgive us and bless you! For the honour of the most honoured one in His Divine Presence, Sayyidina Muhammad ﷺ—*Fateha!* ▲

---

[10]The full *hadith* reads, "Beware of this *shirk* because it is more hidden among my *ummah* than the creeping of an ant." (Ahmad and Tabarani)

13

GUARDING OUR MOST VALUABLE TREASURE

A'udhu bil-Lahi min ash-Shaytani-r-rajeem. Bismillahi-r-Rahmani-r-Raheem. La hawla wa la quwwata illa bil-Lahi-l-'Aliyi-l-'Azheem.

May Allah forgive us! We are firstly in need to ask forgiveness from Allah Almighty because, at every step we take, we are following Shaytan, following the representatives of Shaytan. Therefore, we must look and ask what is the right way, and come back from the wrong way and go on the right way.

The right way goes to endless, eternal life. The wrong way ends in Hells, and whoever falls into Hells, *"La yamutu fiha wa la yahya."*[1] Allah Almighty is saying that those who enter or fall into the fire of Hells, you can't say about them that they are living and you can't say that they are dead. At every moment or even every second, those people, the Fire-people, are dying; at every second, they are dying. And if one second's punishment for one person in Hells were to be

---

[1] *"Neither dying in it, nor living."* (87:13)

divided among all living mankind, all of them would fall down and die.

There, in seconds, death reaches them and they pass from the Fire, and in the same second they come to life and another kind of punishment from the Fire comes to them and they die, and they are in deep darkness, in deep darkness. *La hawla wa quwwata illa bil-Lahi-l-'Aliyi-l-'Azheem!*

People are thinking that it is *asatir*[2]—that what we are saying we have been informed about through prophets is something that is never going to happen. People are thinking in such a way. And that is their imagination.

What Allah Almighty says, *that* is Reality! What we think, it is imagination. We may think but even our imagination can never think what is going to happen to those people if they fall into the Fire, into Hells.

They should say, "We must cry, we must call out to be saved! As much as we are able, we must shout. And we hope that it will be good for us not to be patient and to ask. Shouting and crying, perhaps it is going to be useful; they may hear our crying and shouting. Perhaps mercy may come."

But mercy is never going to reach them. Then they should say, "We must be patient, not to cry, not to shout. Perhaps being patient may be useful for us, and we hope to be saved." But a divine address will come, saying to them, "O people who are in the Fire, in Hells, it is same whether

---

[2]Fable, myth, fairy tale.

you are patient or not patient, never giving you any chance to be saved from the Fire and its punishment."³

Glory be Allah! Here, now, it is so easy during this life—a short, very short time, and there, even the longest life here is going to be like a second, like a second. But people, even for that second, are not going to be patient and follow their Lord's commands!

Allah Almighty is offering and saying to His servants, "O My servants, I am dressing you in the honour of divine service in My Divine Presence. Keep it! For a very short time, keep it, and you should be happy forever." But people think that the life that we are in is endless and no one thinks about his servanthood. They say, "We must establish our work and then we may look after servanthood." And they begin from childhood to be directed towards *dunya*.

All educational systems everywhere are directing students to *dunya*. And all governments, tyrants, are making a rule. If you do not send your children to their schools, if you want to teach them according to your beliefs, they say, "No! You will be punished. You can't do this."⁴

"I am free regarding my children."

"No. You must send your children to our schools to learn the contrary of everything that is heavenly." That is their main aim—to make the new generations not to *ta'aruf*, not to know, heavenly rules. "That is prevented, forbidden. You can't do that. You must follow our orders," and their

---

³*"Burn in it; then be patient or impatient—it is all the same for you. You are only being recompensed for what you used to do."* (52:16)
⁴Certain countries, like the U.S., are, *alhamdulillah*, exceptions.

orders are satanic. If I ask to keep my children and to teach them at home, they say, "No. We will punish you!"

Where can you go? Everywhere that rule is in effect to follow the satanic system, directing all the new generation to *dunya*. "That is the most important goal for you. You must forget everything about heavenly rules and you must follow our rules." And their rules are satanic rules.

And people, when they get older and they begin to think beyond this life, each time they see people dying, people dying, some of them get to be awakened. And at that time, they say, "Oh! I must first finish my task to establish my life, my temporary life. Then I intend to follow what is necessary for the eternal life."

Every time, even though they are getting older, they think of establishing their temporary life and building that temporary life on strong pillars. That is their idea or main aim. And they think, they know, that it is a temporary life, a very short time, but yet they are giving every possibility and capacity that they have been granted to it and making it *"haba'an manthura,"*[5] wasting, wasting that most valuable *jowhar*, treasure—wasting it!

That treasure, people do not use in a correct way. And then they reach an age when they are not be able to do anything because their energy and capacities are always coming down, coming down, and then they are not able to pray, to fast, to keep heavenly rules because they are at the end of their life's physical being, just destroyed, never responding.

---

[5] *"Scattered dust."* (25:23)

If they want to do something, their physical being says, "I can't. I can't move, I can't learn, I can't practice my religion now. I am finished." That person may want to do something but his physical being is not able to do what heavenly orders and rules are ordering him. They can't keep *wudu*; they can't go, they can't walk, they can't talk, they can't learn because their capacities and physical power are coming down, coming down, coming down day by day, and particularly people's physical being becomes different.

Those who are keeping heavenly rules from the beginning, their physical being supports that person, even if he may be one hundred years old. But those who wasted their capacities and abilities and their energies for *haram*, forbidden things, forbidden things have destroyed his physical being.

Therefore, two old persons, one growing older keeping heavenly rules, his physical being is one thing, while another who never took care about heavenly rules, his body is just destroyed because the power of the body, physical being, is in full relationship with our souls, and souls give spiritual power. Spiritual strength is with those who keep heavenly rules, and their bodies must be powerful. Even if they are a hundred years old, still their physical being is helping them and never saying, "I can't do that." They are doing as they did in the younger period of their lives, going on that way. It is not a heavy burden.

On the Day of Resurrection, people will be told, "Prostrate to your Lord!" So many people will be like this, standing, unable to prostrate. Those who never prostrated to their Lord, on the Day of Resurrection they will be unable to prostrate. Instead, they will fall down like a *lauha*, a board, even though their creation is going to be new. On the Day of Resurrection, Allah Almighty will bring them with their new bodies to the place of judgment, but they won't be able—not only here but also when they have finished here, they won't be able to prostrate, to make *sajdah*, to Allah Almighty.

Glory be to Allah, you see that now in our time, in this period, all nations', all governments' educational systems are just built on a satanic foundation—finished. Only a few are getting out free and saving themselves, but the majority are looking at what Shaytan's rules are telling them and following them. Shaytan's rules say, "Run after dunya," and so many billions were just running after dunya and taking nothing with them. They left everything and went, they passed away.

For what are you urging me to run after *dunya*? To reach all treasures, what is the meaning? If anyone was able to carry the treasures of *dunya*, they would find nothing. But they have left everything and gone.

O people, the twenty first century's people, you must change your way! Your way is a wrong way. We are with *Haqq*.[6] Those who are with *Haqq* should reach eternal life, eternity. Those who are not with *Haqq* should be in Hells. No hope for their salvation, ever.

May Allah forgive us and send us what we are hoping for from Heavens, a heavenly person, to gather our hearts on *Haqq*. If hearts do not come to *Haqq*, our physical being can't come. Therefore, we are asking for someone whose

---

[6]Reality, truth.

words will enter the hearts of people, to change their steps from the wrong way to the right way.

May Allah forgive us! Therefore, I am always asking forgiveness from Allah Almighty because ninety-nine per cent are walking with wrong steps. For the honour of the most honoured one in His Divine Presence, Sayyidina Muhammad ﷺ—*Fateha!* ▲

14

THE MAIN CHARACTERISTIC OF EGOS IS PRIDE

A'udhu bil-Lahi min ash-Shaytani-r-rajeem. Bismillahi-r-Rahmani-r-Raheem. La hawla wa la quwwata illa bil-Lahi-l-'Aliyi-l-'Azheem.

The characteristic of egos is to be proud. Everyone likes to be proud, and pride is the main characteristic of egos. And it is biggest hindrance in front of mankind for entering Paradise.

Pride can't enter Paradise, as the Prophet ◎ was warning his nation, his ummah, and saying, "If anyone has even less than an atom of pride in his heart, he can't enter Paradise," because pride is dirtiness. And Satan, Sadanas, Shaytan symbolizes pride.

Therefore Shaytan was thrown out of Heavens. Heavens never accept a proud one; no. That is dirtiness, and Paradise is only for clean people. Pride is the main characteristic of Shaytan, and he wants to give it to everyone. Otherwise, it would be a sleeping characteristic, but Shaytan is trying to make it open and grow and cover our existence.

You may plant a small seed, and if it opens, it becomes a big tree. That seed, if it is in a store, doesn't matter. It never grows. But if you plant it in the earth, then it grows, growing, growing, growing, and becomes a big tree. Therefore, that *dharra*, smallest piece of matter or material, if it is closed, it doesn't give harm, but Shaytan wants to make it to grow. If it remains without planting, it may finally be destroyed, but if you plant it in a field, it will grow.

Shaytan wants to plant his worst characteristic that he used against mankind. He is trying to plant it in everyone's existence. Then, if it grows, it prevents you from entering Paradise, guardians saying, "Oh, who is this? This dirtiness, you can't put it here. This is a dirty person!"

Now there are x-rays, showing. When a person comes to Paradise, they look at him. If clean, he enters; if showing that there is pride in that person, even a little, throwing him out. A person may be a simple one, having simplicity. Simplicity is the way to reach humbleness, humility. A humble person, really humble, he is saved, he is clean from pride. But if a person is not simple, he can't be humble.

To take people to Hells, Shaytan is teaching them satanic teachings, making so many titles, degrees, to make people go up from the first level's simplicity, from humbleness. At the first step, that person begins to say, "Oh, I am someone!" Then humbleness is going to melt. After the first level, humbleness goes away, and Shaytan is trying to do that. Therefore, he is ordering his representatives—and all nations' governments, their leaders, all of them represent Shaytan—asking his representatives to make laws, rules, that everyone must learn.

What do they learn? Through their learning, they learn to be proud. First step, primary school, first class, second class, third, fourth, fifth. When primary finishes, giving a certificate.¹

You have any certificate, Professor ____? You have a primary certificate? O-oh! More than that, secondary? You have a secondary certificate? Oh-h! You, Shaykh ____ — ooh-h! "I have a medal, also, from an architect, *baş muhendis*, chief architect." Doctor, you? "I never leave out any letter of the alphabet on my card."

Eh! Taking up, taking up, taking up, saying "Oh-h!" Then saying, "Who are you? Where are you, that you are saying that we must follow your rules and your orders? We do not see you. No! We are the only powerful ones on earth and authority is in our hands. We do not recognize you and we do not acknowledge your existence. *We* are in existence!"

They² are making me attack their foolish systems of teaching, every time bombarding their false and foolish system, to put it down, to awaken people. Simplicity brings humbleness, humility, and humbleness brings peace to people. But proud ones are increasing. Oh, no more peace, no more peace—Allah Allah Allah! Wrong way!

Islam is a religion of Heavens, coming to teach people that they are in existence through the Lord of Heavens. You are only creatures and imitation titles will never give you any other position. Any other identity, no matter how many

---

¹This refers to the educational systems in Turkey, Cyprus and other parts of the Muslim world.

²See footnote 1.

imitation titles you may reach, never changes your real position, never lets you change from the level of servanthood. But Shaytan is trying to make people cut out servanthood and reach Lordship. And Lordship is only for the Creator.

Shaytan was the first one fighting Allah and wanting to reach Lordship, and he was so eager to reach that point. He knew holy books but he never understood that a person is *mahjuz*.[3] No matter how much someone may learn, it is impossible to reach the final level of servanthood and move to lordship. Shaytan never learned that, and he is trying to make man not to say that there is only one Lord, one Lordship, for all creation, but trying to make people say that *we* want Lordship.

What is that foolishness? Who are you to claim this, while you are so weak? *Wa khuliqa-l-insanu da'ifa.*[4] How are you claiming this, while you are so weak a servant? Don't think that having nuclear bombs or rockets makes you powerful—no! Still you are weak ones. You may use them, your nuclear bombs and rockets, for the *seen* targets of enemies, but there are some enemies that Allah may send to you through your body. You can't see them even under the most powerful microscopes; you can't see and you can't use your rockets on them. *"Da'ufa-l-talibu wa-l-matlubu*[5] *Talib* means *insan*, man; *matlubu* means those viruses or bacteria. You can't see them because they are so small. And from where can you find out their weakness, because those *al'ab*,[6] very *da'if*, most weak, creatures are threatening you, and

---

[3] Confined, limited.

[4] *"And We created the human being weak."* (4:28)

[5] *"Weak is the pursuer and the pursued."* (22:73)

[6] Microscopic organisms.

you can't catch them or put them in prison or kill them? They are so weak, and you, who are claiming "I am powerful," you are also becoming so weak in front of those weakest creatures.

Why are you claiming Lordship? What is that foolishness? But all educational systems are based on it, to make people proud, and pride is not suitable for weak ones. To be proud is only for One, for the *Sultan*. The *Sultan* is proud, *must be* proud; He can't be weak or humble. No, He is proud. His divine attribute is to be proud of everything of which He is *Sultan*. But don't think that, because He is proud, He comes and destroys weak ones.

Men are foolishly claiming that they are *sultans*, and through that title they are running to disturb or to kill weak ones. That is not the attribute of a real *sultan*, and the real sultanate is only for the Lord of Heavens. And He is asking from His servants only to be humble. Humbleness is the most lovely characteristic for weak servants—to say, "O our Lord, we are weak ones. You are Most High, Most Powerful, our Lord." But people, with their diplomas, certificates, think that they have become *something*. They are only learning ignorance, nothing else.

You can't find such knowledge being taught in universities, even in the Islamic world, and more blame for the Islamic world than on others. May Allah save us from following Shaytan, shaytanic teachings, and from following our egos because our egos never want to be humble ones, always asking to be *sultan*, and, *shattana ma baynahuma*;[7] it is so remote for our egos to be *sultan*—impossible!

---

[7] What a difference there is between the two of them.

Only one *Sultan*, and He has absolute sultanate, authority, from pre-eternity to post-eternity, and there is no one else in existence to claim that he is *sultan*. Divine sultanate, eternal sultanate, is only for the Lord of Heavens, the Lord of mankind, our God. And we are His servants.

May Allah forgive us and send us some ones to take people from the wrong way to the right way. For the honour of the most honoured one in His Divine Presence, Sayyidina Muhammad ﷺ—*Fateha!*

The most cheating people are commanders, generals of armies. Therefore, they are using the most important-looking clothes, making so many designs on themselves to show their power, some ones putting swords on their shoulders, some of them putting eagles on their shoulders, some of them putting dragons [laughter], some of them putting crowns, and putting here, also, so many medals, and putting swords, a grand uniform, to make people think that they have become someone powerful. And on the Last Day . . . [laughter]. I don't know if Christians tie their open mouths or perhaps put cotton in them. Muslims are doing like this [tying shut the mouth of a dead body] not to be open, and their eyes, also, doing like this. ▲

15

Training Our Anger

A'udhu bil-Lahi min ash-Shaytani-r-rajeem. Bismillahi-r-Rahmani-r-Raheem. La hawla wa la quwwata illa bil-Lahi-l-'Aliyi-l-'Azheem.

Ghadab means anger. Anger must be. Anger is pressure, blood pressure. When anger comes, blood pressure goes up, and if it is too high, that person going to die.

A'udhu bil-Lahi min ash-Shaytani-r-rajeem. We are running to Allah from Shaytan. Shaytan is full of anger. His anger never settles down. From the day that Allah Almighty ordered the angels, "Prostrate to Adam," he was like a fire figure, and that was his anger.

He was angry with Allah Almighty, *astaghfirullah!* When he was angry with his Lord, Almighty Allah, that fire covered him, and from that time he has been burning, burning and representing fire, and it is continuing. And anger, which we have been given as a grant because we can't live without those powers; anger and sexual power, *shahwah*, must be with a person. When it goes down to the level of zero, that person is finished.

We have been ordered to control these two powers, not to go over their limit or to go over what is necessary for us. If we go further, it will destroy the person physically as well as spiritually. Must be under control!

And the second power, the sexual power that a person must have in himself, it is a grant, also, and we have been ordered to take control of it, as well. If you aren't able to control it, that power will also take you to dangerous areas and big accidents. Then that person is going to be finished. They must be under control, these two powers, the two that are the real sources of our physical being's life. Without one of them, our life is finished. That person is dead.

Allah is ordering us to be in balance. You must use that power of anger within its limits, not to go high because it is a dangerous area, as well as not to come down too far. That is *dhull*,[1] to be unable to do anything, to be under the feet of someone.

Defense, for everyone, passes through that power. Above its normal level, we may use it for certain purposes, but it is a dangerous area. And to use that power at the lowest level and below it, it is also dangerous for everyone, killing us physically and spiritually. You must use anger in that balance.[2]

---

[1] Meekness, submissiveness, insignificance, lowliness, humiliation.

[2] That is, not to leave its expression uncontrolled so that it produces violence or cruelty, nor to stamp it out so entirely that one accepts oppression and victimization of oneself and others.

And that is the reason why, when a person came to the Seal of the Prophets, the most honoured one in the Divine Presence, Sayyidina Rasul-Allah ﷺ, asking, "O our Lord's representative, Rasul-Allah, *ausini*.³ Tell me something to hold on to for my safety, for my benefit, to be in safety, here and Hereafter, not to be harmed and punished," the Prophet ﷺ said, *"La taghdab* — don't be angry."⁴

"Don't be angry" means "Control your anger." If you leave a horse without reins, that means no control. It may take you into dangerous areas, since normally the reins control your mount. And if you leave your ego, whose creation is just similar to Shaytan's — fire — it may take you to a dangerous area.

Therefore, the Prophet was saying, "Don't be angry." That means, "Try to be able to control your anger or you will finish." As many times as the man said, *"Ausini, ya Rasul-Allah,"* asking for advice, he repeated it, saying, "Control your anger."

With what may you be able control it? What are the reins of ego? The *Shari'ah*, heavenly orders, is the reins of your ego. If you do not use that rein, your ego will kill you, destroying your personality physically and spiritually. Ego never knows joking; it never makes a joke with you, no. No mercy from your ego to you, and no respect, also. Don't expect respect from your ego to your real being.

Therefore, you must keep the *Shari'ah* as reins and *tariqah's* orders as a whip. If not understanding with reins, you must use the whip of *tariqah*. If not, finishing —

---

³Direction, instruction, order, advice, admonition.
⁴Bukhari.

physically destroyed, then spiritually making you less than zero. *"Ulaika kal-an'am"*;[5] those people who do not take care and leave their egos without reins, they are like animals. *"Bal hum adal,* no they are worse" if they leave it without using either heavenly orders or *tariqah* orders, they will never leave the level of animals, making that person come down.

Therefore, the *Shari'ah* keeps us from coming down to the level of animals, keeping men's level above the level of animals. If you use the *Shari'ah*, you keep the reins on the level of mankind. If not using it, falling down, and at the same time, if you do not take care about *tariqah* orders, you will go down still more to the lowest level, below the level of animals.

Therefore, anger is from Shaytan, a satanic characteristic. The same characteristic is with your ego, and you are in need of someone to train it. If you want to ride on a horse but you aren't able, you find someone who trains horses. By yourself, you can't learn it. That one will teach you.

Therefore, every Muslim, every believer, must have at least one trainer, training him how to ride his horse. But Shaytan is playing with the minds of Muslims now, first of all, Arabs, and among Arabs, Wahhabi people are rejecting the most simple thing. If you want to ride on a horse, you are in need of a trainer. What about if you want to ride on your ego, not to have your ego riding on you? But they are saying, "No need!"

---

[5] *"They are like cattle; nay they are worse."* (7:179)

How can it be? And I am seeing on roads, here and in London, in Europe, many cars with "L" written on them. What does it mean? "Learner." For a car, you need a teacher to teach you, to learn how to drive it—a car, such a simple thing and you need someone. What about for guiding your ego? But they are saying, "No need, no need. *Shirk!*"

From where are they bringing that *"shirk"*? Which book is writing this? If I want to learn from someone how I can ride my horse and make my horse go, run, towards the real goal of our lives, how is respecting my teacher and obeying him going to be *shirk*? What is this foolishness, what is that? Really they are such foolish people, destroying Islam, with money opening so many centers, Wahhabi centers, *"d'awa"* centers.[6] They are only destroying Islam. May Allah change theirhearts!

You need a *mu'allim*, a teacher or trainer. Also, I see that even football players have trainers to teach them how to play. What about for you? You are not in need? Why do you open schools and appoint teachers, professors—*why*? They are teachers. Why do you not make an objection to that?—"O people, you are doing *shirk* because you are listening to that one. No need! Leave him! You can learn by yourself."

Who learns by himself, without going to high school or university, only looking at their books and learning—who is that? But Wahhabi people think that people can learn everything through their books. Can't be!

---

[6]Centers for the propagation of Islam.

May Allah forgive me. Therefore, this important point that They are giving me permission to speak about is anger. For anger, that makes people be in existence, in real existence, with the honour of mankind, with the honour of being from human nature, for the honour and respect of being deputies, representatives, of the Lord of Heavens on earth, this is the way.

May Allah forgive me and bless you! For the honour of the most honoured one in His Divine Presence, Sayyidina Muhammad ﷺ—*Fateha!* ▲

16

CONCERNING SPIRITUALITY AND MATERIALITY

A'udhu bil-Lahi min ash-Shaytani-r-rajeem. Bismillahi-r-Rahmani-r-Raheem. La hawla wa la quwwata illa bil-Lahi-l-'Aliyi-l-'Azheem.

Yauman jadid, rizqun jadid.[1] Each day comes *"kal-fulki-l-mashun."*[2] Each day comes with new things, each day comes with unexpected events. No one can know what tomorrow will bring, and today, also, we do not know now how this day is going to end. From now up to evening, there are still four or five hours.

Countless events are coming, individually and collectively. That shows the greatness of Allah Almighty, because each one has a private destiny. Never are two destinies going to be the same. Can't be!

And that is the reason why the Creator, the Lord of Heavens, our Lord, Allah Almighty, is impossible to be understood—impossible! We are such weak ones, we are such

---

[1] New day, new provision.
[2] *"Like the laden ship."* (36:41)

small ones. Let alone a person of one-and-a-half or two meters height—if the figures of any or every one of mankind were to be as big as this huge universe, not two meters tall, but anyone, everyone, of such hugeness, still their minds could never carry the greatness of the universe.

He, Almighty, can create everyone in such a way. He is able, and He is not in need to use material. no. Material is for you, for your understanding, but in the Divine Presence there is no material and no existence for anything. He can create millions or billions and trillions and quadrillions like this huge universe by an order. He would only say, "Be!"[3] which means, "Come into existence!" and it would be ready.

It would be ready, and for its existence, in our sight, in our knowledge, there would be material, but in front of Him, nothing. It is only an order—an order; no need to use material for creating. He never uses material for universes, for Heavens, no. If using material, that material must be from Him, and He is never in need of material because His existence does not depend on material. But the beings of everything in existence depend on material.

Therefore, material is for creatures, but the Creator never uses any material for creating. He only uses an order. No material, no projects [chuckles]—no projects for making the Heavens, for making something with projects and using material. He, Almighty, only uses His order, saying "Be! Come into existence!" and finished! That order, according to His Will, just comes into being and appears. But you can't touch it.

---

[3] "*Kun!* Be!" The divine Word of command, mentioned in 2:117; 3:47, 59; 6:73; 16:40; 19:35; 36:82; 40:68.

WE HAVE HONORED THE CHILDREN OF ADAM

Sughuri Hazretleri,[4] one of our Golden Chain's grandshaykhs,[5] Abu Ahmad 'Abdur-Rahman al-Sughuri, was saying, "I have been in Hijaz for *Hajj*[6] thirty-seven times. Seven times I was there with my physical being, material existence, and thirty times I was present at 'Arafat[7] with my spiritual being." And in that spiritual being there is no material.

People think that this physical being is most important. No! Important is your spiritual being. *It* is important, not this material being; no. Your spirituality has no material, no. And he was saying, "Sometimes people met me in Makkatu-l-Mukarramah or in 'Arafat and said, 'O Shaykh, welcome to you! How is it? You were making making *du'a*[8] [in Daghestan] with us for the *Hajj* pilgrims when we wanted to leave for the Ka'bah, the House of the Lord—you were making *du'a* and sending us off. We left you in Daghestan. How are you here?"

And he was saying, "O my sons, after you, another caravan came and called me, also, 'Come with us,' and I came with them."

---

[4]*Hazretleri*: a Turkish honorific title for individuals of high spiritual rank, such as *Sahabah* and *awliya*.

[5]The chain of the grandshaykhs or *awliya* of the Most Distinguished Naqshbandi Sufi Order, going back to Abu Bakr as-Siddiq and through him to the Holy Prophet..

[6]Hijaz: the province of Saudi Arabia in which Mecca and Medina are located. *Hajj*: the annual pilgrimage to Mecca, one of Islam's five "pillars" or obligatory acts of worship.

[7]A vast plain some miles outside Mecca which is the site of one of the principal rites of *Hajj*.

[8]Supplication.

When they were trying to take, to kiss his hand, he did not give it, saying, "I have *'udhr*, an excuse, for my *wudu*.⁹ Don't touch to my hand," because, if they did like this, they would find nothing. People might be frightened, and therefore he did like this and did not give his hand to them because it was only an appearance without material. Therefore, "*Yas'alunaka 'ani-l-ruh. Quli-r-ruhu min amri Rabbi.*"¹⁰

When people asked the Seal of Prophets to tell about our spirituality, our souls, Allah Almighty was saying, "O my beloved one, say to them that it is an order from my Lord. It is an order, and you can't understand."11 You can understand only material beings, but beyond that, you are never going to understand. It is only an order for your physical being. All worlds and creations, all of them, have material, different material, for their creation, for their physical beings, but for their souls, no. Allah Almighty does not use material for our souls.

Therefore, souls and our physical being are never going to be same, and the *jaddal*,¹² arguing, is never going to be ended between soul and material being. Material being wants to be the boss, and spiritual being says, "No, you can't be. You can't be my boss because what I am carrying of divine power, you don't have. You don't have that power because the material world, everything that belongs to

---

⁹To avoid breaking *wudu*, for as a follower of the Shafi'ii madhhab a woman's kissing the hand will break a man's *wudu*.

¹⁰"*They ask you [Muhammad] about the soul. Say, 'The soul is by my Lord's order.'*" (17:85)

¹¹A paraphrase of 17:85 above.

¹²Argument, dispute, debate, quarrel.

materiality, is in limits, but what we have been granted through our souls is not in limits."

Therefore, our power through our souls reaches to the ends of creation. And the power of our souls in such a state may be present everywhere because souls are never limited by material being. Souls' area, their fields, are unlimited, but our physical beings' fields are only within a very short and small area.

That makes people lose the essence of their real being. They do not understand that we have a physical being that is never going to be in existence without material. And there is another existence within ourselves that is our spiritual being, and that is never in need of material and never going to be in limits because it is an order from Allah Almighty.

Therefore, no one can reach real knowledge about the Lord of Heavens till they reach the real understanding of their spirituality. Through spirituality, you can touch ("touch" means you can reach some knowledge about the Creator), but don't think that your material being can think about it and be able to bring true information about the Creator. Therefore, people now are asking, "How is Allah? Where is He and where was He, and up to where is He going to be?"

Those are nonsensical questions because it is not your area of responsibility to ask as long as you are imprisoned in the material world. You must cut it. When you cut this prison, you may find yourself in a world where there is no materiality, only spirituality; and you can't bring any description of spirituality, no. Anything you can bring for the understanding of spirituality, material being never understands. It is impossible; no. This is something, *that* is something else.

With your material being, you can't understand your spiritual being. Therefore, you must try to melt it, to destroy your material being, either here or after death. Then you should find yourself in an ocean of spirituality that belongs to Allah Almighty's Will. When He is going to say, "Come into existence!" it will come, and that existence of our souls may be understood by our spiritual being. And your spiritual being, as our Grandshaykh was saying, is going to be like a drop coming from the clouds and reaching the ocean. It *becomes* an ocean. You can't find it, you can't bring a limit for it. It has just reached an Ocean that never can be known.

Therefore, men, when trying to reach Allah Almighty's Divine Presence, are in need of some training, some practicing to break down their material being and for that drop that is in your material being to be free. As that drop comes and enters the Ocean, it is going to *be* Ocean. But you need to break down that material being. Material being, no room for it in existence. It is an imitation existence, but the soul that comes, reaches the Oceans of Unity of Allah Almighty without hindrance and disappears.

May Allah give us good understanding for His knowledge, to be able to understand. As long as you are surrounded by materiality, it is impossible to approach the understanding of our Lord's divine position. Therefore, we are asking and trying to reach that point and to save ourselves from the heaviness and darkness of materiality, to reach peace and contentment, and the oceans of lights, oceans of power, in His Unity Oceans.

May Allah grant it to us, and bless you and forgive me. For the honour of the Seal of the Prophets, Sayyidina Muhammad ﷺ—*Fateha!* ▲

17

"NOTHING CAN GO OUT OF ITS PRIVATE LINE TO ITS DESTINY"

A'udhu bil-Lahi min ash-Shaytani-r-rajeem. Bismillahi-r-Rahmani-r-Raheem.

Kullu amrin bi-waqtihi marhun;[1] everything appears in its time and its space or place. Nothing happens in this world each day but that for every happening there is a private time. It must come in that line, and it is either going to finish or to begin.

In twenty-four hours, each day 24,000 appearances[2] are coming, and from among 24,000 appearances everyone takes his share. And each appearance comes in its private line and time. No one gets involved or comes and makes an accident; no. Everything is in its private path and appointed time, and must appear in its prepared space or place and must go on it. And when it finishes, a second happening must take its *dawr*, turn. Therefore, everything, under heavenly control, appears or disappears. In, out; during units of

---

[1] Literally, Everything depends upon the time [that Allah] decreed for it.
[2] Divine manifestation.

time, billions of happenings go in, billions of happenings go out.

But our world is seen as if it was as before, unchanged.. Never, never! It has changed. It changes, also, because it has been used by this world, something taken and something given. At every time there is a change, and nothing is going to happen before its time or to be delayed.

"*La yastakhiruna sa'ata wa la yastaqdimun*"[3] — everything that we are saying is in this holy verse. It is not only for our *ajal*,[4] our last moment, last breath; no. It is for everything. "*La yastakhiruna sa'ata wa la yastaqdimun.*" Nothing is going to get out of its private line that is its destiny.

For everything there is a destiny. Must be a beginning, must be an end, and that beginning, *la yastakhiruna sa'ata wa la yastaqdimun.* You can't reach it beforehand and you can't expect it after its appointed time. That is Allah Almighty's greatness, that you can't reach to understand anything about, and this that we are speaking about belongs to *af'al-Allah*, the Essence of Allah Almighty. It is in deep darkness. No one knows the real being of Allah Almighty's Essence, so that for His Name, in that position, we are saying only "*Huwa*".

"*Huwa*" means unknown — unknown. If there are no stars in the sky at nighttime, you couldn't understand the skies or space. When these lights appear as lights in the darkness, you understand about that darkness. Without

---

[3]"*[And when their term arrives], they will not remain behind an hour nor will they precede [it].* (7:34, 10:49, 16:61)

[4]Appointed time, moment of death.

them, you can't understand anything about darkness because darkness means you can't see.

You can see in the daytime by the sun. If no sun, you couldn't see anything of the sky, and at nighttime, when the sun has set, you can't see anything. These artificial lights never give you anything. Only by the lights of stars in the sky can you understand, can you know that something is there. You can understand that there is deep darkness, and those are signs. If not, you couldn't see anything, and if you couldn't see, that means you couldn't know anything, couldn't understand anything—no understanding, finished. Therefore, in the daytime and at nighttime, you need lights from Heavens to see. Think about it. These artificial lights give nothing to you. If in the daytime there were no sun and at nighttime no moon or stars, you wouldn't see. And if you didn't see, you could never understand the existence of anything.

Therefore, Allah Almighty, for His Essence, manifested on His deputies Divine Attributes that belong to Him. Those Divine Attributes make you understand the existence of that One, Huwa. If Allah Almighty did not show or send information about His Divine Attributes, His Essence would be unknown. His Divine Essence can be known only according to His Divine Attributes. The Divine Attributes are lights that make you understand that their lights come from somewhere.

A candle without wax, a lamp without oil is not going to shine. No; it is dark. When putting wax or oil, those candles or lamps show you something. And Allah Almighty puts some signs of His real Essence that are seen as lights. Those lights signal the existence of Someone who is unknown.

You may see a lighted candle, nothing more. You can't see how it is in existence or how it gets to be lighted. Those attributes are indicating, and they are signs, also, of the real existence of the Lord of Creation, the real existence of the Lord of Heavens, the real existence of Allah Almighty—only signs.

From those Divine Attributes come His Holy Names, written on them Names, appearing Names. And we are the first level. Selected or chosen ones, they know the names of lights, as everyone looks at the nighttime skies but they do not all know the names of stars. Only chosen people know that that is the Pole Star, that is the Bear Star, that is Scorpion, that is the Bull, Taurus, that is the Scale, that is the Fish, that is Aries. Only twelve *buruj*,[5] twelve main signs for understanding our sky, *sama'*, twelve, *dhati-l-buruj*. "*Wa-s-sama'i dhati-l-buruj*."[6]

This is for description. And you do not know, but special people who know about it, only they can tell their names. And the Divine Attributes, also, not everyone knows. Chosen people from among mankind who have a relationship to Heavens, one foot on earth, one foot in Heavens may understand, may read it, "That is this," and they can tell us. Therefore, not everyone knows about Divine Attributes, and they may say "Hayy". That is the divine attribute, *hayat*, life—His divine attribute, Hayy, means alive. They may say the Name to you.

The Holy Names have come as a description of the holy Divine Attributes. Those Names are understood by chosen

---

[5]Constellations, signs of the zodiac.

[6]"*By the sky, having constellations.*" (85:1)

people who have inherited heavenly knowledge through the heavenly, chosen servants of Allah Almighty, prophets, coming and bringing *af'al*, actions. Everything of actions belongs to them. Never-ending, those actions coming from these Names that belong to the Divine Attributes, which are signs of the unknown Essence of the Lord of Heavens.

What we are saying now is that all things, even every atom, are within the actions of those Holy Names of Allah Almighty. Holy Names are arranging the actions of all things, of everything that appears here: when it is going to appear and when its period is going to finish, showing the real beginnings of everything and the real point of endings; in which area it is going to happen, at what time they are going to appear.

Therefore, we must know that sometimes—not sometimes; every time—"*Wa kana-l-insanu 'ajula,*"[7] we want everything to be quick. No. It must wait for its time, the beginning and ending. When coming to an end, no one will get it back—no, finished. But man wants everything to be so quick, and "so quick" can't be. Therefore, the most important sign of servanthood is to be patient: to be with Allah and His divine Will, not to put our will into it but to follow His Will. That is real respect for the holy commands of Allah Alighty.

"Be patient," He is saying. He knows when it is going to finish. He knows when it is going to begin because every finishing brings a new beginning. Ending and beginning, leave it to the Lord of Heavens. That is the real sign of serv-

---

[7] *"And man is ever hasty."* (17:11)

anthood, that you are giving a perfect kind of servanthood to your Lord, to your Creator, Allah Almighty.

Therefore, Islam came to teach people their relationship as servants towards their Lord—as He is the Creator, how our relationship as servants to our Lord is going to be. That is all. All holy books are only bringing that essence, but people have lost it and they are running in nonsensical directions. They have lost the way, and when they lose the way, they are falling into troubles and problems, and they are punishing themselves through themselves.

May Allah forgive me and bless you! For the honour of the most honoured one in His Divine Presence, Sayyidina Muhammad—*Fateha*! ▲

18

"CONTENTMENT IS A TREASURE THAT IS NOT EXHAUSTED"

A'udhu bil-Lahi min ash-Shaytani-r-rajeem. Bismillahi-r-Rahmani-r-Raheem.

It is an Association. We are coming here, asking to be good servants. That is our goal, and everyone's goal must be that—to be a good servant to his Lord and to be a good one for people on earth. All holy books have come with the same point that I am speaking about now, and the summary of all holy books is what I am saying now: to make people good servants to their Lord, Almighty Allah, and to do their best for each other. That is all.

But as long as Shaytan is alive and he is not retired, he never gets to be tired and he runs after people to make them enemies to one another. Now people are not looking if they are from the same nation, from the same religion, from the same beliefs. They are only thinking about themselves, how they are going to enjoy themselves with their physical desires. The entire or main aim for them is to fulfill their physical desires, that is all. And they know that fulfilling physical desires is with money, with material things.

Material things are one thing, but enjoyment is not a material aspect, a material thing—no. A person may be a billionaire (not with Turkish liras, no; may be a billionaire with dollars, riyals, euros, *eeee*-euros, pounds), but he never enjoys himself because so many reasons are making people not to be in pleasure, not to enjoy themselves—so many reasons. What I am saying is that a person may be a trillionaire—not with Turkish money, with *their* money—and he may do everything for his pleasure, but there is some thing that is a reason for his not reaching full pleasure.

A person passed away last week in Turkey. He was a billionaire in dollars, also, and he had every *fursa*, every chance, to enjoy himself. But there is a bad characteristic of people, a bad characteristic of our egos. What is it?

Envy; envy, *hasad* or being jealous. A man may be a trillionaire but he sees that there is another person who is also a trillionaire. "Why is he a trillionaire? Why? I think he has more than me. How can I get that person to be taken away? I must think about it. I must prepare some tricks to make that person come down."

Each day the *borsa*, stock market, shows that one's *tahwil*, exchanges. "His shares are going up, my shares are coming down!" Cursing, cursing; "May Allah take that person from our line!" So many; it is not only one. So many people I am seeing. That was enough to make that person unhappy, and at nighttime thinking about it, during the daytime always thinking about it. "What is happening to my stocks? .My shares are coming down and his shares . . . ? What is happening?"

That is enough. A person is a trillionaire but he is never happy because so many people are in the market, money market, business market, stock market—so many people. Finished! Trillions never give any pleasure to that person, finished.

Therefore we are saying, contentment, satisfaction and enjoyment, and pleasure and peace in the hearts is something else. It is not a material aspect, and material aspects never bring a person to that point, no. Rather, people think that if they have more money they should reach the top level of enjoyment. That is Shaytan's influence on them, finished! That is the main aspect for these people now living everywhere on earth, and shaytanic teachings are cheating them and they are never going to be happy and in peace and enjoyment—finished! Maybe a person who has only daily wages gets little money but he is working, he is happy. But billionaires are not happy.

Therefore, religions that have come from Heavens[1] are teaching people true ways, but people are rejecting them and coming to the wrong way—the wrong way. The Prophet was saying, *"Al-qana'at kanzun la yafna."*[2] *"La yafna,"*—to be satisfied with a small amount gives people peace, and it is also a never-ending, never-finishing treasure. It is a real treasure, *qanu'a*, to be satisfied within a person's self with what he has been given or granted, because there is no meaning in collecting billions or trillions—no meaning, never giving any enjoyment and never giving any benefit to people here or Hereafter.

---

[1]Meaning the three faiths based on divine revelation through prophets, Judaism, Christianity and Islam.

[2]"Contentment is a treasure that is not exhausted." *(Hadith)*

That is an important point, but people now have left the real aspects, real goals of their creation. Therefore, we are saying that the best thing is what prophets brought, teaching people or calling people to be good servants. Run after servanthood, not after *dunya!* No; try to be a good servant, an excellent servant, in the Divine Presence. That gives you contentment and peace. *"Ala bi-dhikri-Llahi tatma'ina-l-qulub."*[3] Allah .Almighty is saying, "Everyone who is with Me, never forgetting Me, keeping Me in his memory, I am giving him refreshment of life, and peace and contentment and enjoyment." They are such happy people. Even though they may wear only one shirt with a *sharwal*,[4] trousers, they are happy—they are happy.

Once our Grandshaykh was in Damascus, Sham ash-Sharif. I was with him and we were passing through a market. So many people were selling and buying. There was a *kaldırım*, pedestrian's walkway, on this side, and a person was sitting there

He was sitting on the ground, on stone, nothing under him, on the pedestrian walkway. In front of him there was a *karton*, newspaper or such a thing, on which he had put his wares, what he was selling and buying for his provision,, making a display, like this. And I saw what was on it, also.

If I gave you one hundred dollars or one hundred pounds or one hundred euros, you would not take out of the dustbin those pieces that he was selling. [Laughter.] Old nails, old *jilets*, razors, and *ilac kutusu*, medicine boxes;

---

[3]*"Unquestionably, by the remembrance of Allah hearts are assured."* (13:28)
[4]Arabic for *shalwar*.

then, for coloring shoes, empty bottles of shoe polish, and old keys—so many things. .

Şeyh Efendi[5] was asking, *"Nasıl ticaret?* How is your business going today?"

He was sitting like this. Then standing up, saying, "Oh-ho, excellent, Shaykh, excellent!" [Laughter.]

"Anyone coming and looking?"

No one could! If Doctor ____ were there, he would use one bottle of alcohol to wash his hands because of so many bacteria on them. If I gave you one hundred pounds, you would not take it. Doctor, if I gave him two hundred, he would never take it to take them to the dustbin! "All microbes, bacteria; leave it! Put some alcohol on it!"

"What alcohol? I am a *tajir*, I am a merchant. How is it? Oh, first class!" That person had contentment. Those billionaires, trillionaires, no contentment!

Subhanallahu-l-'Aliyu-l-'Azheem! People are never listening to heavenly advice but listening to Shaytan, and Shaytan is never going to make people happy or in contentment. And we are looking, and people are running to kill themselves, to finish. All *jahd*, efforts, are to invent new types of weapons to kill people. And Allah Almighty is saying, "Don't kill, don't kill! Don't injure! Don't do harm." Allah is saying this, and Shaytan is saying, "No, don't listen. Kill, injure, harm people, so that no peace comes on earth!"

---

[5]Grandshaykh 'Abdullah ad-Daghestani.

May Allah forgive me and bless you, and give us a good understanding so that we may put a limit on our desires. Desires are always going, running in front of a person and the person is running after them. And his *ajal*, his death, is always near him but he is running, wanting to jump over the death-line to reach such nonsensical goals.

May Allah give us good understanding so that we may be good for His servanthood and good for mankind, for creatures and for creation. For the honour of the most honoured one in His Divine Presence, Sayyidina Muhammad ﷺ—*Fateha!* ▲

19

AVOIDING HEAVENLY ANGER THROUGH GOOD SERVANTHOOD

A'udhu bil-Lahi min ash-Shaytani-r-rajeem. Bismillahi-r-Rahmani-r-Raheem.

By the name of Allah, All Mighty, All Merciful, Most Beneficent and Most Munificent. Glory be to Allah! *Subhan Allah, Sultan Allah!* Real sultanate is for Allah only, and He is *Sultan.* Everything belongs to Him, everything is from His creating.

He creates, bringing from unknown worlds and sending to other unknown worlds, and those worlds also belong to Him. You have only an appearance in a mirror, or, better than a mirror, we may say the screen of a TV. You may see on the screen of a TV from East to West, from North to South, so many countries, oceans, mountains, jungles, animals and unknown areas, different colours of people, and everyone is appearing in his private or special appearance.

You can't find a person exactly like another one. For everyone, Allah Almighty uses two eyes, one nose, one mouth, two ears, one head, one face, and these elements that He uses—eyes, nose, mouth and ears—have countless appearances. No matter how many people there may be, their noses are going to be different, their eyes are different, their ears are different, their mouths are different, and then you see that it is a different face, *Allahu Akbar!*

Do you think that a painter, an artist who paints, may be able to paint more than, we may say, seventy different faces? Seventy different faces, do you think he can paint? It is difficult. Perhaps he may paint seven faces. Then he is going to wonder about the eighth face or to wonder how he can do another painting for ten different faces or more, so difficult. That is the meaning—that man's capacity, ability, is going to be nothing, but Allah Almighty's Power makes millions and billions of people not to be alike. Each one is in another shape, form or design.

He is *al-Musawwir*. That means "Designer". He is the Designer, and He can make endless, countless designs, *Allahu Akbar!* For the Power of Allah Almighty and His ability or capacity to do everything, He is not in need of thinking in order to design, no. You must think and then you can draw, you can make a design, but He, Almighty Allah, does everything by His Order.

What is His Order? To say "Be!" When He orders something to be and says "Be!" that must appear. If He says "Don't be!" then everything is going to disappear. And He is the Designer with His unlimited Power. Daily, He designs the lives of people. However many billions of people are living on earth now, on the world—worldwide continents, worldwide oceans, and countless creatures on it—the design of this world today is not the same as it was yesterday. No, that design has finished, and today another design has come.

Today, the design, with its countless activities, actions, works, appearances is not going to be like yesterday's design; no. Today's works are just one hundred per cent different. No way to keep something from yesterday as it is today, no. It has just passed away, and tomorrow there will also come another appearance of creation or design on earth that is not going to be same as today's, no. Everything has changed. And you are seeing on TV so many things passing, going; passing, going; coming and going.

The first time I looked at TV when it first came to Cyprus, some people were looking at that big box and so many things were appearing. And a peasant got up and went to the back and looked to see if anyone was behind it.

"Where is that person? Not inside?"

"Yes, inside."

"But I do not see him."

I said, "It is closed."

People thought that someone was inside. Now everyone knows that that screen brings so many, countless appearances, and when you are turn it off, nothing appears. And, *subhanallah*, Allah Almighty gives authority to man to use one power, electricity. If that does not run into it, nothing is going to appear.

But we—we have much more perfection [than any technological invention??]. This TV is a man-made instrument, and Allah Almighty gives man the capability to use a power from nature, which is electricity. The twenty-first century's technology, its life is with this electricity, that no one knows what it is. What is running through these wires they do not know. If they say, "These ions are moving," if not moving, these technologies never work. This never-ending *something* running in it, that is a secret power that Allah Almighty just granted man to use for his benefit.

But Shaytan is making men not to use it for their benefit but instead to use it to harm others. All technology is only used for shaytanic purposes. Everywhere, technology is getting more power from electricity to destroy and to kill and to do to harm to people because Shaytan is teaching them, "You must harm people. Don't give your benefit to people but harm them as much as possible."

That is the shaytanic way. And Allah Almighty is saying, "O My servants, try as much as possible to give your best, to do your best in everything." That is the heavenly teaching, but Shaytan is saying, "No, try to do everything to harm people, to destroy everything on earth, not to give peace to people. Make them be in fear!" That is shaytanic, and all religions have come to make people be good servants to Allah and good ones to one another.

This is the summary of heavenly messages in which the Lord of Heavens is saying, "O My servants whose servanthood I am accepting in My Divine Presence, try to be excellent servants to Me!" How? What do you think? If a person is employed by a sultan or a king, do you think that that person does not try to do his best for the sultan or that he never takes any care? He tries to make the sultan or king more pleased with him.

That is what our intellect says. Then what about for Allah? To be the servant, obedient servant of a king, those people want to continue to do their best for their king or sultan to make him pleased with them. I never heard that a person does the contrary of that and does his worst, because if he is does his worst, he is going to be kicked out. "Be the worst one for his service" is not what our intellect or our mind says to us, never saying that. Rather, our intellect says, "Try to be most obedient and trustworthy in his royal presence." So what about for Allah, who created you? Why are you not taking care of His servanthood?

Do you think that the twenty-first century's people are obedient servants to their Lord, or even thinking about it? Never! You can find only a handful of people on that way, and others are saying, "I don't care! I don't care about service, about divine service."

"What *do* you care about?"

"I care about my teacher who is giving me a Ph.D., Doctor Shaytan."

Shaytan is becoming "Doctor" now, Ph.D. In the twenty-first century, Sadanas is becoming "Doctor". Ph.D., Master's, he is giving now. Whoever follows him, he gives them that diploma, that honour, the honour of being his best employees, of being his best servants.

But really they are not his servants, they are his slaves. Slavery is something and servanthood is something else. Servanthood gives honour to a person, slavery takes away honour. And Shaytan has just made the whole nation of Muhammad ﷺ in the twenty-first century his slaves, and there is slavery everywhere. What Shaytan is saying they follow. They never keep any respect for their Creator, the

Lord of Heavens. What do you think is going to be the future for these people?

And we are speaking on an important point—that from the beginning of prophethood, prophets' teaching has rested on only two pillars. The first is that they called people to try to be the best servants to their Lord, and the second is that they called people to be good ones to each other and to give their best to everyone. As much as possible, you must give your best to every creature and you must not harm anything.

We are looking at an ant. If you want to kill it, it runs away, afraid of being killed. Without its harming you, you are going to kill it, while He created it and it has a private position in creation.

Nothing is created for nothing. Everything is created for something, for some purpose. You can't say, "Why was this created?" No. You don't know, but the Creator knows, and therefore He created that.

People are on the wrong way. They are following shaytanic teachings that say, "As much as possible, harm people, give trouble to them, be trouble makers," because the first troublemaker, who was it?

The first troublemaker was Shaytan, Sadanas. When Allah Almighty ordered, "Prosrate to Adam," he said, "No!" making trouble among all the angels. The angels were ashamed of what he did in the Divine Presence, saying "No!" The first troublemaker was Shaytan, and every kind of troublemaker is a shaytan, *sadanas*.

That is the shaytanic teaching that is bringing the whole world now to the edge of Hells. O people! You have been ordered to be from mankind! Keep you honour, and your honour is to be the best servants in the Divine Presence. And when you are the best servants of the Lord of Heavens, blessings come on you, and those blessings give life to this earth and everything on it. But if you do not give your servanthood to your Lord, curses come, and curses give harm to everything on earth. May Allah forgive us!

Once Sayyidina Musa ﷺ was passing through a village. And he entered and found a spring running with such cold and sweet water. He drank and made ablution, and he was so happy to be there and passing through.

Everything was green—the land, the meadows. People's faces were shining; their animals, cattle, were so happy, so healthy, and they were breathing such clean air. Everything was good and he was so happy. And he went on.

After a time he was thinking to come and see that village again. And he came and looked. "Where is that village? Have I come to the wrong place? But I know that I came through that same way, and there is no other village in this area. But what has happened? The spring is no longer running; there is no more water here, no more people; and the trees are dried up and everything is in ruins."

And he said, "O my Lord, what happened? You know what happened to these people here, where they went, how their village was destroyed."

And Allah Almighty answered, "O Musa, it is the same village. But once there came a person who did not take any care of My obedience and servanthood. He came, passing through, and he drank from this water.

"My divine anger and curses came on that person and on the people who welcomed such a person, and I made that spring dry and everything to be dried up. I took away My blessings from them and curses came on them. This is the same village where you were before."

And now, what are you saying? People are not taking any care of their Lord's obedience; everyone is running away, everyone is thinking only about their *dunya*, this life, nothing else. They are not taking care of their Lord's obedience, they are not taking care to be good servants of Allah Almighty, and therefore curses are coming on them.

Every time you look at this TV, you see explosion, explosion, explosion; people dying; earthquakes, floods, storms and fires; and also countless illnesses coming on people. One finishes and another unknown curse comes on them. Therefore, the way for mankind to be saved from heavenly curses and to reach heavenly blessings is that they must say, "Our way now is the wrong way. We must change this wrong way to the right way." Otherwise, all of them are going to finish.

And now there has begun a cleaning. It just began, and everyone who does not take care that their souls are clean should be taken away, not only a few. "Oh-h, ten people died, fifteen people died, a hundred people died."

Leave that! Even millions is not going to be a correct count of the people who are going to die when curses come now. I am running to Allah, to His shelter, to be sheltered because billions of people are going to die now—billions, not millions! Out of six, one will remain and five are going to be taken away. He knows! He knows who is harming people, who is harmful for people, and He will take them away. Good ones will remain, bad ones will go.

May Allah forgive us and give us a good understanding of heavenly messages. It is also written in the Old Testament, the New Testament, the Psalms, and finally in the last Message from Heavens, the Holy Qur'an, telling the same point to people: to be good servants, not to be Shaytan's followers.

May Allah forgive us so we may be in safety! For the honour of the most honoured one in the Divine Presence, Sayyidina Muhammad ﷺ—*Fateha!* ▲

20

CONCERNING "MODERNIZED ISLAM"

A'udhu bil-Lahi min ash-Shaytani-r-rajeem. Bismillahi-r-Rahmani-r-Raheem. La hawla wa la quwwata illa bil-Lahi-l-'Aliyi-l-'Azheem.

Allahumma, alhimna rushdana wa a'idhna min shururi anfusina.[1] May Allah Almighty protect us from the tricks and traps of Shaytan. The biggest danger for a person is to be heedless because a heedless person may be caught by a trap or may be cheated by the tricks of Shaytan. And we are in need, because Shaytan always wants to cheat us and steal our faith, our *iman*.

The Seal of the Prophets, the most honoured prophet in the Divine Presence, Sayyidina Muhammed ﷺ, was saying that Shaytan has just *muqatti'u-l-amal*.[2] No hope remains with Shaytan that the people living in Mecca and Medina, *sharafahum Allah Jallahu 'Ala,*[3] will come back to worshipping

---

[1] Our Lord, inspire our guidance and we seek refuge in You from the evil of our selves.

[2] Cut off his hope.

[3] May Allah, exalted be His majesty, honour them [the holy cities].

idols—finished! But Shaytan is happy if he makes their people do some other bad things besides worshipping idols.[4] Even though it is not like worshipping idols, he is happy if he can make people walk on the wrong way, as now people are cheated.

The Islamic world is just cheated. Muslims are not saying, "We are Christians or Jews or some other religion," but they are followers of the Western lifestyle. Shaytan is cheating them and insisting that Muslims must try to be "westernized Muslims." Otherwise, Western people may say to you, "You people are not on our level. Your level is always under our level. You should always be *muta'akhir*[5] You can't be like us, and we represent modern civilization. You will never reach it as long as . . ." They do not say, "As long as you are Muslims," but they say, "As long as you do not follow us, you are not going to be on our level."

"What can we do?" our first-class square-headed leaders and doctors are asking. "What can we do?"

They are saying, "You must reform, you must examine your religion because your religion belongs to fourteen centuries ago, but now we are living fourteen centuries after Sayyidina Muhammed ﷺ. Therefore, you must think about it if you want to come to our level. You must try to leave your religion's principles," and Islam brought some principles that are unchangeable. But they are saying, "You must

---

[4]Similar to the Prophet's saying, in his last sermon, "O people, Satan despairs of ever being worshipped in this land of yours, but if he is obeyed in matters short of that, which you consider of little account, he will be pleased. So beware of him in your religion." (Muslim, Tirmidhi and Ibn Hisham)

[5]Behind, backward, underdeveloped.

change it, you must change it! You must take away some pillars. Pillars that are principles, you must take them away, and then you should be like us, on our level."

Last 'Eid[6] in Turkey, in Konya, on the first day of 'Eid al-Adha, a building eleven stories high, in seconds, all of it came down.

How did it happen? They are saying that the first floor was a big gallery, to be used as a showroom or a big store or something like that, and they were renting that place to a company. That company saw that it was a large area, an eight hundred meter sized place. What did they say?

This is something that happened to put in front of the eyes of Muslims what they are doing, *subhanallah!* "*Faqsusi-l-qasasa la'allahum yatafakkarun,*"[7] Allah Almighty is saying. "You must relate some happenings, some events, so that people may think about it." And They are just giving me this to speak to you about.

It was an eight hundred meter hall, and there were so many columns or pillars. The one who was renting it said, "These columns are no good. We must take them away to make a big, big store so that when people come, these columns will not cause any trouble for looking right and left." And they took away all the columns that that building was standing on, and suddenly, after that—no pillars, oo-h-h!— that big building, eleven stories, came down, eleven stories becoming five, one coming on top of the other.

---

[6]One of Islam's two major festivals.
[7]*"So relate the stories, that perhaps they may reflect."* (7:176)

Europeans are saying, "You must leave some things from your religion. Take away some columns, to be modernized Muslims, like us. You must take some pillars from it. As they came, we shall take them away."

Europeans are saying, "One of the pillars is to pray. Leave it! The second pillar, fasting, no need. Another, *zakat*[8]—everyone is working; no need. *Hajj*[9]—for what, *Hajj*? Take a holiday, going and coming. Why are you going to go? That, people's going to Hijaz, it was for a holiday,. And then you should be modernized Muslims.

"And instead of what you are saying, '*La ilaha illa-Llah, Muhammadu Rasul-Allah*' ﷺ, say, 'Father and Son and Holy Ghost.' Come and say it! We can draw and also paint their imaginary pictures. Look! That is the Father, that is the Son, that is the Holy Ghost. Look! You are saying 'Allah'. Where is Allah? Show me Allah! Look, we can show you. Look!"

And our heedless people are saying, "Oh, we'd better look and do like this, like that; like this, like that; like this, like that." And now they are making a drama about Jesus Christ, and the whole world going up and coming down And it is far from Reality, imagination!

Those who are going to Western countries, their system of education is based on that falsehood. And it is also coming to the Islamic world, and saying, "You people are still living fifteen centuries earlier. You must change everything, you must be modernized-headed people." And they are taking away the pillars one after another, one after another.

---

[8] The third pillar of Islam, the prescribed poor-due or charity.
[9] The fifth pillar, pilgrimage to Mecca.

That is Shaytan. Shaytan is saying, "I am very happy if I cheat people and they become outwardly like non-Muslims."

"What are your beliefs?"

They may say, "Islam."

"What are your prayers?"

"No prayers."'

"What is your way? The Islamic way?"

"No, the modern way."

"Now you are getting to be like us. If you do not do this, you will always be below our level." This is a big cheating of Shaytan's, and I am sorry to say that the Islamic world is just falling into such a terrible position. They are destroying themselves by themselves!

Everywhere, first in Arab countries, they are enemies to each other, and inside, Shaytan is making them to be *shi'ah*, so many parties, and to fight each other. Here, there is the Cypriot Turkish government. We are only a handful of people, but they are saying ten parties, fighting each other. And making them worship idols, also.[10]

O people, you must be awake! Wake up, O Muslims, wake up, because dangerous and very terrible and horrible events are facing you, and you see what is happening in the Islamic world, everywhere killing each other, explosions. If

---

[10]That is, through the many pictures, statues and sayings of Ataturk displayed throughout Turkey and Cyprus.

they were real Muslims or real followers of Islam, Allah would never send Christians, non-Muslims, on them. Don't think that non-Muslims can be supporters for you—no!

Don't be heedless! That heedlessness is bringing every kind of trouble on Muslims and Muslim countries and the Muslim world. When they are going to put back Islam's pillars, to make its pillars stronger, then they should be sheltered by Allah Almighty. If they do not take care, Shaytan will take them under that columnless building and the whole building will come on them, and then they will disappear.

We believe that Islam will be renewed because Allah Almighty promised that to His most beloved one and most honoured servant. He promised, and also gave *basharat*, good tidings, about the future of Islam. Allah Almighty is saying, "*I am the protector of Islam.*[11] *I* am keeping it, and no one can destroy its structure. What they are doing, they may do. '*Wa makaru wa makarullah.*'[12] They are trying to take Islam away, using every kind of trick and trap, but *I* am keeping Islam because Islam belongs to Me, and I am the Protector, the Shelter. *I* am sheltering."

What is this that soldiers hold? A shield for Islam. Everything that comes on the shield never touches real Islam. "I am the Protector, I am the Guarantor of the Holy Qur'an, I am the Guarantor of Islam. They can't touch it. No, no! They may do everything, but finally it will all come on them and they will regret."

---

[11]"*Indeed, it is We who sent down the Message, and indeed, We will be its guardian.*" (15:9)

[12]"*And they plotted and Allah plotted.*" (3:54)

They are destroying themselves, like the Egyptian people. They built a big dam to prevent the Nile from running freely, wanting to make it under their control—a big dam, a high dam, *sadda-l-'Aliyi. Nil mubarak*[13] did not say anything. "Doesn't matter, put your barrier on me. I am looking for the holy command of my Lord to take away the high dam and those who built it, and their cities, also—to carry them to the sea, as Allah Almighty carried Pharaoh and his soldiers into the Red Sea."

Leave them! They may do. Their 'dams' are so weak now that they are trying to stop Islam, and the power of Islam is so great. They are trying to stop it, and Islam is *sakin*, keeping quiet, never objecting to it. Let them build! Let Europeans, let Christians, let Jewish, let *meza kurto*[14] people do what they can. They may build anything; they are trying to stop Islam. Build! Now there is coming such a power that, if there were not one Christian world but seventy Christian worlds were building, in one minute they should be taken away—*whoo-oo!*

Allahu Akbar! Allahu Akbar! Allahu Akbar! 'ala kullu man takabbbar wa tajabbar.[15] Therefore, heedless Muslim people, now they are on the side of Christians, *min taraf al-Christians??]*[16] They are looking and claiming that their

---

[13] The blessed Nile.

[14] "*Meza kurto*, a Greek word, means "not belonging either to Islam or to Christianity. You can't say whether this is a Christian or a Muslim," Shaykh Nazim explains.

[15] Allah is greater than all who are arrogant and tyrannical.

[16] On the side of Christians

safety and their success and their *mustaqbalat*, future, is to be with the Christian world. They should be taken away, with the Christian world; those people who are running with Europeans and non-Muslims and the Christian world, they should be taken away. And a handful people here, on this side, is saying, "We are not following Christianity, we are not modernized Muslims. That is only a deceptive word that they are using, 'modernized Muslim.'"

"Modernized Muslim"—that means "Christian Muslim." But the same person can't be Christian and Muslim. No, they are lying, and they have been cheated and they are at the same time cheating the Muslim world. But the Lord of Heavens is looking. There is coming such a power that, in a minute, their barriers to prevent Islam from going to East and West, to North and South should be taken away.

Allahu Akbar! Allahu Akbar! Allahu Akbar! Don't look at what is happening now. Everything that is happening and that you are seeing is against Muslims. If they were real Muslims, never would such *mu'sif*, sorrowful, events happen. Couldn't be! We must ask forgiveness from Allah and we must come to the safe side, the Islamic side, not to be cheated.

May Allah forgive me and bless you! For the honour of the most honoured one in His Divine Presence, Sayyidina Muhammad ﷺ—*Fateha!* ▲

21

THE SOURCE OF PLEASURE AND PEACE IS CONTENTMENT

A'udhu bil-Lahi min ash-Shaytani-r-rajeem. Bismillahi-r-Rahmani-r-Raheem. La hawla wa la quwwata illa bil-Lahi-l-'Aliyi-l-'Azheem.

We are keeping the way of the Masters, may Allah bless them, and through their blessings His mercy may reach us, also.

We are in need of blessings from Allah Almighty. When He is happy with His servant, He sends His blessings on him. If He is not happy with His servant, He does not send His blessings. And if blessings do not come, curses come. When curses come, that person never going to be successful here and Hereafter, and he can't be in safety here or Hereafter.

Safety is the most important factor in our lives. If a person is in fear, that means he is not in safety. If a person is in safety, there is going to be satisfaction in his heart and fear can't be. Fear can't be for those people who are in satisfaction because they feel safety and protection from Allah Almighty.

Therefore, we have a saying in Islam from our traditional knowledge, *"Al-kha'inu khaifun."*[1] That means that when a person keeps what he promised to Allah Almighty on the Day of Promises,[2] he feels satisfaction within himself, and when satisfaction comes, fear leaves. But those who are not keeping their promises, *kha'in*, they are going to be in fear and they can't feel contentment in their hearts. They are always full of fear.

And when fear runs through the heart of a servant, his life is going to be bitter—bitter, no taste. A fearful person may eat something but he can't get pleasure from eating because there is fear in him. And those who do not keep their promises in the Divine Presence, fear must be in their hearts and their lives are never going to be safe lives, no. Always they are afraid. He may be a president, he may be a king, he may be a prime minister, he may be the richest one, the biggest businessman, but fear is always hurting him and never letting him taste the pleasure of this life.

Don't say, "No pleasure in this life," no. There is pleasure here and Hereafter for those who keep their promises and their Lord is pleased with them. When their Lord is pleased with them, their life here should be a peaceful life and they must be in pleasure. A person may even eat only dry bread, may even drink salty water, may even live in a small hut, may even live under a tent, may live in a desert,

---

[1] "The disloyal/false/faithless/treacherous *[kha'inu]* one is afraid."
[2] Referring to 7:172.

but even if he is in prison, he tastes pleasure. He never gets to be displeased, even in prison, jail.

Sayyidina Jacob's son, Joseph, Sayyidina Yusuf ﷺ was in prison for so many years, but, because he was pleased with his Lord, Allah Almighty granted him pleasure even though he was in a terrible jail. Sayyidina Yusuf was in prison but he was with Allah, he was with his Lord.³ If you are with your beloved one, with your darling; it is not important whether you are in a palace or in a jail because important for a person is that he is with his darling. He wants his darling. "O my darling!" Yes? Eh! If no darling with you, if I put you in Buckingham Palace, you will say, "I am asking for my darling, but she or he is not here. What am I going to do with this palace and its furniture? No!"

The first man, our grandfather Adam ﷺ, was in Paradise, and he was going around. Everything, every beauty, was in Paradise, but the Lord knew that he was unhappy, no pleasure in his heart. He was not pleased to be in Paradise. He was looking at palaces, looking at trees, looking at jewels, looking at such beauty in Paradise, but it did not give him full pleasure.

Then, for some seconds, even for one second, even for one-third of a second, there came to Adam, from Allah Almighty, not sleep but being absent from himself. If a person is asleep, he is not in himself, with himself, leaving himself and sleeping. And during a very short time, a kind of sleep came to Adam ﷺ, and then he awoke.

---

³12:37-37-38.

In that moment when there was no clock or any measure for measuring that unit of time, Allah Almighty created our grandmother Eve. Then Adam opened his eyes and looked, and he was full of pleasure. He felt that he had just reached the pleasure and satisfaction that he had been wanting. A hundred per cent contentment came to him, and he did not look at any other beauty in Paradise, no. His eyes only went to her, saying, "That one, that one, is now filling my heart with pleasure." And he said, "Come!"

And our grandmother said . . . [Body language; laughter.] Yes. Paradise was full. Even if there had been nothing of Paradise, his heart was just full of our grandmother's beauty, making him so pleased, so full of pleasure. If they had been in a prison, they would not have cared whether they were in jail or in a palace.

Now, this is a world to which Allah Almighty sent our first grandfather and grandmother. And Adam and Eve were happy, even to be on earth; and this is the world of troubles, the world of problems, the world of evil, the world of devils, but they were happy. In spite of everything that hurts people, they were happy with each other. They felt that now we are in Paradise, real Paradise, because our hearts are just in contentment and full of love, and her beauty is enough, more than enough, in place of the beauty of all the gardens and palaces of Paradise.

Therefore, this is a *tamthil*, an illustration, to people that if a person is with his beloved one, he may be anywhere and he should be happy and in pleasure. If he loses his beloved one, if you put him in palaces—not here, even in Paradise—he is not going to take any pleasure. Therefore, Allah Almighty gives pleasure to His servants here and Hereafter. The pleasure that Allah Almighty's beloved servants are finding here makes them be in Paradise here; but those who are not happy with their Lord, with their Creator, everything gives them trouble, makes them displeased, and their hearts are full of fear.

And therefore, there is pleasure in this life, not for those people who have billions of dollars or pounds or euros. Those millions or billions never give pleasure or make them pleased here. But even if they eat broken and dry bread, they may be like the Companions of Sayyidina Muhammad ﷺ, who ate only one or two dates in twenty-four hours and no bread, even dry bread, and they were happy people, they were pleased, and they felt that they were in safety because they were with their beloved one.

O people, try to understand the message, heavenly message. Try to understand the meaning of prophethood. You must try to understand for what prophets came or for what they were sent. Then you should find a new atmosphere. When you go in it, you can be pleased, you can be in pleasure; you should be happy, you should be in peace.

If you understand what was the main purpose of sending messengers from Heavens to those who are following heavenly people—those who are always connected from earth to Heavens—you will enter a new atmosphere in which you will feel the taste of life with pleasure and with being pleased. If not, there is another atmosphere. If people go into it, they may be the richest ones or most powerful ones on earth, but their atmosphere is going to be like a prison for them. Even if they have billions and palaces and power and titles, their atmosphere is one kind and believers' atmosphere is something else. Believers may taste the pleasure of life. Unbelievers, they taste the difficulty and bitterness of life. They are always in troubles, sufferings and in miseries.

O people, look again! Your life is going to reach an end. Before your life comes to an end, see which atmosphere you are living in. If you are not happy, that means you are on the wrong way and in a poisoned atmosphere.

Change your atmosphere! At any step you take, if you want to change from a bad and poisoned atmosphere to a good atmosphere, you may change, you may find an exit. For reaching the best atmosphere, Allah Almighty makes an exit at every step. In only one step, you can change your atmosphere to a good atmosphere. You should be happy, throughout your life you should be happy! When you leave this temporary life, you should be pleased. When you are buried, you should be pleased. When your soul is taken from you and sent to the Divine Presence, you should be happy.

May Allah bless you and forgive me! For the honour of the most honoured one in His Divine Presence, Sayyidina Muhammad ﷺ—*Fateha!* ▲

22

"DON'T PONDER OVER ALLAH BUT PONDER OVER HIS CREATION"

A'udhu bil-Lahi min ash-Shaytani-r-rajeem. Bismillahi-r-Rahmani-r-Raheem. La hawla wa la quwwata illa bil-Lahi-l-'Aliyi-l-'Azheem.

We are nothing. Allah—glory be to Allah!—is Powerful and there is no limit for His power, never giving anything of Himself and never taking anything from Himself.

If He were to give something, that would mean that He can be in pieces,[1] He is not something whose existence has pieces, no; He is One. He is One, Number One—among numbers, Number One. If you give something to One, it changes; it is no longer One. If you take something from One, also, One disappears. Therefore, One never accepts to give or to take. His existence, His personality, can't be like any other thing. Impossible!

And from pre-eternity to post-eternity, Allah Almighty is the Creator. He creates. Don't think that when

---

[1]Separable parts.

He creates something, He gives to His creatures from His Essence, no. If He gave, He would be like us. We can take, we can give.

The most difficult thing is to think about His Oneness, the Oneness of His *varlık*, existence. To think about it is the most difficult. As an example, no matter how much a man may think, he can never understand about the being, the real being, of a female, and also a female can never understand about the real being of a male. It is impossible for a man to understand the situation or position of a woman, and also for a woman, it is impossible to understand the real being of a man. If you want a female to understand the situation of being a man one hundred per cent, that woman must be a man, or otherwise it is impossible. And a man, if he wants to understand the situation of a woman one hundred per cent, that one must be a woman.

And this is true for everything. That is a palm tree, never understanding a *kayısı, mişmiş*, apricot tree. If understanding, it must be an apricot tree. This an apricot tree, that is another apricot tree, but they are not completely alike, the same, no. This is one, that is another one. Yes. That is a plum tree, that is an apricot tree. A banana tree can't be an avocado. If anyone asks, "Who is 'Abdul-Karim?" he must be 'Abdul-Karim to understand who 'Abdul-Karim is.

All things that He created are creations, creatures. For creatures, it is impossible to understand *how* the Creator is—impossible! To understand the Creator, you must *be* the Creator, and it is impossible because this universe can't have two Creators, it can have only one Creator.

What is creation and what are creatures? You may think about that but you aren't able to think about the Creator. He is the Creator, creating, and His creation is never-ending. Leave off thinking about the Creator. You may think about creation, not creation as a whole but the creation of creatures that are in existence. He is the Creator. He can fill this universe or other universes like this universe. Hundreds or billions or trillions or quadrillions of times He can create and this space is never going to be full. This is space. If our Lord, the Creator, wants to bring into existence, to create, a universe quadrillions and quadrillions of times this size, this space is never going to be full, "full house." And if He likes, He is able to put all of them, billions and trillions of universes like this universe, into the space of an atom. Don't use your balance[2] for Allah, O heedless people! Don't show me icons! People are painting and saying, "This is God," *astaghfirullah!* Yes; He may create billions and trillions and quadrillions and quintillions like this universe and order them to be in an atom's space, Allah Allah! There must come a crack in people's heads if they think about it.[3]

Don't think! *"Tafakkaru fi alai-l-Lah wa la tafakkaru fi dhati-Llah."*[4] You may think about creatures but not about the Creator. Don't try to think about Him, no. How can you put your mind on that when such a universe, millions and millions, may be in an atom's space? It is easy for the Lord of Heavens to say "Be!" in that space. Finished, and they

---

[2]Measure, scale.

[3]That is, people's brains will crack from the futile effort of thinking and trying to understand Allah's Essence, Power, Knowledge, skill and His divine workings.

[4]"Think about Allah's favors/blessings/benefits but don't think about Allah's Essence."

are ready in an atom's space, and no *ziham*, no crowding. Everyone may freely take their places, and they should be so happy. They may say, "Oh-h-h, such a big space! Oh-h!" Therefore, think about creation or about all creatures. And He is the Creator. You may look at creatures, and through His creatures you may understand something about their Creator.

Therefore, we are saying that He does not give or take even atoms' existence.[5] When He creates, He does not take anything—*His* creation!—and also He does not give anything. It is only His order, "Be!"—"Be!" and it is going to be, to appear and to take its place in that area, and to say, "I am here, O my Lord. Glory be to my Lord!"

Everything is glorifying Allah. Such countless universes and creatures, all of them are calling out, shouting and saying, "Glory be to our Lord!" They are shouting, they are shouting their praise!

It is only an order. An order is not a material thing. Your mind is never going to understand *how* that order is, *how* that order brings billions, trillions, quadrillions of units of space, universes, into being.

Your imagination can never reach it—impossible! And everything that you think about to understand our Lord's order and command, His saying "Be!"—that is all imagination and Reality is beyond that. Therefore, you can't understand *'alamu-l-amr*.[6] His dominion of power or the

---

[5] Neither putting anything of His Essence into creatures nor taking anything of them into Himself, but simply creating by the divine word of command, "Be!"

[6] The sphere or domain of Command.

dominions of His Power Oceans are impossible to be understood. You can never move more than an atom's distance.. You aren't able.

You understand? Our souls can understand, and whatever thing our Masters are saying, don't think that they are addressing your physical being. Physical being understands nothing, but They are aiming at our spirituality, and our souls are swimming in those unknown Power Oceans' dominions.

That is our limit, and beyond that limit you can't reach. Even your imagination can't reach past that limit. Each time you move towards real Power Oceans' dominions, you should find yourself moving with that atom as a vessel moves through an ocean. Although it cuts distances, it is always in that Ocean because you are in a ship, and that ship is always moving through those countless Power Oceans' dominions. No matter how much you may move, you can't reach beyond that ship, always in it. It is impossible to leave that ship and enter into Power Oceans' dominions.

This is addressed to the 21st century's people who think that they have reached the top limit of understanding of this world and they want to reach beyond this planet. They are never satisfied now to be only on this planet. They have some deep desires, strongly wanting to move beyond this planet, to know what is there, but they can't reach. By themselves, they can reach from one distance to another only on this planet.

They want to move beyond this planet, but they are going to be finished. Their existence is going to be at the point of zero, no more existence in this universe. They want to move and to understand, but they can only use this planet, and they can look at where this planet is going. But they can't see; they can't see because materiality never lets mankind move from this planet to beyond this *kehkeşan*,[7] galaxy.

You must try to reach another distance while you are on this planet. If this planet were to move beyond the solar system, then the solar system would move beyond our galaxy, and when leaving this galaxy, you would look and see billions and billions of galaxies.

How can they reach the end of galaxies? That means that it is impossible to reach beyond our imagination. All of them remain in our imagination. And Reality is the same as that *wali*, saint was saying: "Allah Almighty, Allah—He is Allah. *Hua al-an kama kan.*"[8] The Lord of Heavens, He is as He was from pre-eternity up to post-eternity, and you can't find a way to reach that *manzar*,[9] view—to reach beyond this creation and look.

You can't cut that distance to reach the end of creation and see who is Allah. It is impossible. But this desire, deep desire, teaches men to ask for what is beyond their level and to move through countless distances, through countless levels, through countless horizons, to find the last horizon and to reach Reality. And it is impossible.

Therefore, now, mankind are falling into trouble because they are not thinking about such huge subjects, and they are coming, turning to themselves. They should find

---

[7][Tr.], Milky Way.
[8]"He is now as He [always] was."
[9]Sight, appearance, view, panorama, perspective.

everything within themselves, but they are running to find everything outside of their existence. And it is impossible.

Your existence is not a real existence. You must turn back to the One who gives you that existence by His command and makes you appear in an atmosphere whose ends you can't reach because it is also swimming in the countless Power Oceans of divine dominions.

May Allah forgive us and make us think about such high matters, and leave useless things, not wasting our valuable lives that we have been granted as a chance from Him to think about it and to move into those areas that no one is going to understand. But their understanding is constantly continuing from their distance, and then they should be happy with that movement, through their creation, from level to level. *"La-tarkabunna tabaqan 'an tabaq."*[10]

You should reach, through your creation, from one horizon to another, from that horizon to another,[11] and your pleasure, your lights, are going to be more and more and more. You should be with your Lord's Divine Presence as it is appointed for you even through an atom's space.

The dominions of the Lord of the Heavens are, *alhamdulillah*, we are saying, unlimited. If they were within limits, men would always be in sadness because one day that would finish; but real pleasure for mankind, who are

---

[10] *"You will surely travel from level to level."* (84:19)

[11] *"We will show them Our signs in the horizons and within themselves until it becomes clear to them that it is the truth."* (41:53)

deputies and created to be, on behalf of their Lord, patrons on earth, gives us countless pleasure. If those dominions were to be in limits, men would disappear or finish under the darkness of sadness. They would never taste anything. But the Lord of the Heavens has countless dominions of Power Oceans, as well as countless dominions of His Divine Attributes.

May Allah give us something for understanding, to be in pleasure here and Hereafter. For the honour of the most honoured one in His Divine Presence, Sayyidina Muhammad ﷺ—*Fateha!* ▲

23

THE GREATNESS OF THE GRANT OF OUR CREATION

A'udhu bil-Lahi min ash-Shaytani-r-rajeem. Bismillahi-r-Rahmani-r-Raheem. La hawla wa la quwwata illa bil-Lahi-l-'Aliyi-l-'Azheem.

By the name of Allah, All-Mighty, All-Merciful, Most Beneficent and Most Munificent, the Creator, giving all things their creation. If He does not give them creation, nothing is going to appear in existence. From the smallest particle of matter, its existence is a grant from the Creator. Its creation is a grant, a grant whose greatness you can't imagine. If the imaginations of all people came together, they wouldn't be able to imagine it.

The greatness of that grant is according to the greatness of the Creator, not looking at the smallness of creatures, no. "*Al-hadiya bi-miqdar muhdiya.*"[1] You must not look at that gift, that grant. It may be just an atom. Don't look at

---

[1] The gift corresponds to the measure of the giver.

the amount or *qadr*[2] of that grant, but you must see from whom it is coming to you.

The *sultan* may send one cent, one *piastre*, one pence, one penny to you. If you have perfect understanding, you are not going to look at what has been sent to you, but you must be happy because it is a grant from Allah Almighty to you, and you must make its value like the value of a Paradise, if you were to be granted a Paradise.

Because we are always *naqsan,* imperfect, imperfection in mankind makes man look at the size or look at the value, *miqdar,* the amount of the grant. That is imperfection in man. Perfect people never look at that gift and its amount, but they see from whom it is coming. From Allah Almighty it is coming, and the receiver should be so happy.

That is perfection in a person, to see from whom that grant is coming to me. *Allah Allah, Allah Allah!* It is not the same, if some person gives you an orange, as a *sultan's* giving you an orange. No; can't be. It is the same—one orange, one orange—but its value is according to who sent it to you, from whom it is coming to you.

An orange is coming to you from the Lord of Heavens, or I may give one to you. I am putting boxes there. If anyone comes, I give everyone oranges, but because I am nothing it has no value. But He is our Lord. If He sends it, its value is another thing. The same orange that was sent by the Lord, by the *sultan,* its value is so high, but if an orange comes from a common person, its value is something else.

---

[2] Or worth, value, rank.

We Have Honored the Children of Adam

I was in Turkey in 1940, sixty-four or sixty-five years ago. I went to a shop where they sold some drinks, old-style (at that time, no Coca-Cola, Such-a-Ma-Cola). I saw in that shop a glass, written on it—now there are people making his statue and worshipping him—that once *he*[3] came there and drank a drink from that glass. Therefore, they put that glass on a golden *maq'ad*, pedestal. And I was surprised. That was an ordinary glass but it was valuable among people because that one had drunk from it, giving such value to that glass, and they were eagerly trying to keep it, to protect it.

Therefore, anything coming from the *sultan* is valuable, and, according to the *sultan's* rank, it becomes more valuable. A big *sultan's* grant is more valuable. Something may be given by a high-titled person, but a king's grant is something else.

Creation is a grant from the Lord of Heavens. Even if that creature is only one atom, it can't be in existence by itself. Creation causes things to come into existence. Therefore, existence is really a grant from the Creator.

All things know this and they are glorifying, and their glorifying never stops. *"Wa in min shayin illa yusabbihu bi-hamdih."*[4] All things are glorifying Allah Almighty because He granted them to be in existence, and existence can't be given by anyone except Him. Only He grants it. And they know this and they give their highest glorifying to their Creator, Allah Almighty.

---

[3] Kemal Ataturk.

[4] *"And there is not a thing except it exalts [its Lord] with His praise."* (17:44)

We, mankind, are heedless creatures, not thinking about our Creator. Particularly in our time, we are the most heedless ones in all historical periods. From the beginning up to today, there has not been any nation, any people, like the ones living now because they never give any time to think about their existence and to say, "Thanks be to our Creator, Allah, the Lord of Heavens!"

They are such heedless ones! From the beginning up to today, every nation took a little bit or more or the utmost care to give their highest respects and highest glorifying to their Lord. But in the twentieth century, and now in the twenty-first century, people are so far from thinking about it. They are such heedless, such ignorant ones, and such dark-hearted people. Perhaps their levels are going to be below the levels of rocks.

Rocks know, and they say, "*Subhanallah,* glory be to Allah!" but people living in the twenty-first century do not say this. They do not take any take care or say, "Thanks be to our Lord, glory be to our Lord! And this existence is a grant from the Lord of Heavens to us, and our being is the most perfect in creation among creatures."

They do not even think about it. They are running after computers, they are asking to leave their abilities, to be *mu'atal.*[5] They are trying to make every ability that Allah granted them not to work, and they are trying to make some instruments to give every ability, which is a big grant to mankind from Allah Almighty, to those machines — computers, Internet, FAX.

---

[5]Out of work, inactive, inoperative.

"We have so many computers! We can count how many galaxies, how many stars, how many suns, how much distance." They are all lying; it is all imagination! *"Wa lakin shubihi lahumhalouhu;"*⁶ they are imagining. They are trying to make themselves only for their egos, to feed their donkeys. They do not want to give their donkeys straw. Instead, they are trying to give them baklava.

Baklava, you know baklava?—a sweet, that famous sweet coming from Aleppo, from Beirut, from Damascus, from Egypt. But if you bring and put in front of a donkey a *sini*, tray, full of the best sweets and also put there straw, the donkey will come and look [laughter], never eating the sweets but eating the straw. And particularly for old donkeys that have no more teeth for straw, their owners are making soup from straw and ground barley and a little bit of flour, and putting it. If you put good *kebap* here [laughter], it will come and drink that soup, very happy!

Now people, the twenty-first century's people, are feeding their donkeys with soup, never tasting from this best, best food. Therefore, the twenty-first century people's level is going to be below the level of animals. Animals do not change their nature. They do not eat sweets but they want to drink soup of barley with water, without cooking, even. If you put salt, also, they should be very happy.⁷

---

⁶"It was made to appear so to them." (4:157)

⁷Here, Maulana adds facetiously: "If you want to come to look, it may kick you with two legs because you are *rahatsız ediyor*, disturbing it when it is drinking and you comr. Two legs—*trak!* I heard that it was written in a newspaper that a person disturbed his donkey, and the donkey bit his hand and broke three bones. Very angry when they are eating and

Yes, sir. These people, the twenty-first century's people, are foolish ones. There is a university. University students have no money, no food, no place to sleep, and they are coming to learn at the university. And I am saying, "*Yahu!*[8] What are you doing? Finally, if you finish, what you are going to get?"

The university should give them a black hat and finally a paper, saying, "This is a diploma for you. Take it! You learned *something*."

I am asking, "What did you learn?"

He is saying, "Nothing," putting on the hat and taking a photograph.

"Do you know Allah?"

"No."

"No rights for Allah?"

"No."

"Do you know what are the rights of people?"

"No."

"What is the aim and goal of mankind?"

---

you come! They think that you are coming to be a partner with them, to share, and then they kick you."

[8]Turkish expression, meaning approximately "See here!"

Knowing nothing. "What is the benefit of this world, this universe? From where did it begin, where will it end?" Not knowing. "And who is its Owner?"

If you ask, he will say, "We don't know."

May Allah forgive us! O people, give more glory! Glorify your Lord, Almighty Allah! He is not in need of your glorifying but *you* are in need. You must give high respect, the highest respect, to your Lord, to make Him pleased with you that He granted you to be in existence—the biggest, biggest grant from Allah Almighty because His kingdom is endless, His dominions are countless, His Power Oceans are without end. Try to gain His pleasure, to say to you, "O My servant, come! I am accepting you for My divine service in My Divine Presence. I am accepting you. Come!"

Where are these people going? The twenty-first century's people are the most heedless people, most ignorant people. May Allah take that ignorance away, because ignorant ones are in darkness, and whoever is in darkness is full of fear, and if a person is full of fear, he or she is never going to taste the good and pleasure and peace of this life or after this life.

May Allah forgive us and bless you! For the honour of the most honoured one in His Divine Presence, Sayyidina Muhammad ﷺ—*Fateha!* ▲

24

THE ENDLESS HONOR ALLAH GAVE TO THE CHILDREN OF ADAM

A'udhu bil-Lahi min ash-Shaytani-r-rajeem. Bismillahi-r-Rahmani-r-Raheem. La hawla wa la quwwata illa bil-Lahi-l-'Aliyi-l-'Azheem.

It is an Association. Allah Almighaty addressed the Seal of Prophets, the most honoured servant in the Divine Presence, Sayyidina Muhammad ﷺ. From the Heavens, the Holy Qur'an came to his heart and the divine addressing came through him to his nation. Allah Almighty addressed him for his nation and for all mankind in his time and up to the Last Day, the Day of Judgment, Resurrection Day, and he spoke in His words to all mankind.

A *sultan* addresses one person with his royal command, royal order or royal rules. He tells the grand *wazir*, and the grand *wazir* tells it to all the citizens of the sultanate. There is no need for the *sultan* to call everyone and to speak to them one by one; no. One person is enough; from one to all. If that one is not there, then it can't be. The *sultan* is never going to address anyone individuallybecause his position is not suitable for coming to the level of his citizens and to speaking to them; no.

Therefore, *sultans* kept to themselves, not going among common people, because they had a glory and greatness that belonged only to themselves. If coming to the level of common people, they would lose their greatness and glory. Common people would say, "Oh, this one is also like us. Why? What is his position, to be over us, and why are we under his command? Why are we bowing to him?"

You are not bowing to the *sultan* but you are bowing to the position, to his royal existence. You are not bowing to that man, but what he represents, you are bowing to *that*. He represents the real Royal One, he represents the Lord of Heavens, His representative.

Therefore, ignorant people were saying to each one of the prophets, and saying to the Last Prophet, also, "Oh, that one is like us. He goes through the streets, through the markets;[1] he does what we do. How can he be above our rank?" They did not look at what that Last Prophet represented, the rank in which the Lord of Heavens had dressed him of His greatness and glory. You must prostrate to him, as when Allah Almighty created Adam ﷺ and ordered all the angels, "Prostrate to Adam," and the angels immediately prostrated. They understood the rank in which Allah Almighty had dressed Adam and they knew that he had been dressed in Allah Almighty's glory. They looked, saw, and quickly ran and prostrated. They never looked at his physical being, no.

---

[1] 25:7, 20.

"Adam, *I* created him. *I* am that One who created Adam with My Hands."² That must be well-known. Among all creation, Allah Almighty never gave that honour of making a being by His Divine Hands except to the father of mankind. Angels, no. Angels were created by His order, but Allah created Adam's being by His Divine Hands. That is glory, and that was only given to Adam. And afterwards, all his descendants are taking their share of that honour.

Angels know that they are created by divine command, Allah saying "Be!" and they come into existence. They belong to light worlds, coming from lights, divine lights. In seconds, millions, trillions are coming; no need for Allah Almighty to make them, their being, with His Divine Hands. That was granted only to Adam. And He dressed him from His glory and put from His divine crown on his head. And the angels were looking when Allah Almighty said, "Prostrate to Adam," immediately falling down and making *sajdah*, prostrating to him.³

---

²38:75.

³See 2:34;7:11-12;15:30-33; 17:61; 18:50; 20:116; 38:73, 75 for the story of Allah's command to prostrate to Adam and Satan's rebellion. Here, Shaykh Nazim adds: "Sayyidina Yusuf ﷺ, Joseph, had a dream when he was a young boy, and in his dream he saw that his twelve brothers, his father and mother, were prostrating to him. Why? At that time, that divine crown [of prophethood] was just put on Yusuf's head. Therefore, all the others looked and fell down prostrating to Yusuf ﷺ, not to his physical being, but he represented the Lord of Heavens' glory. That glory was just dressed on him." The story of the prophet Joseph is narrated in entirety in the twelfth *surah*, *Surah Yusuf,* one of the most fascinating chapters of the Qur'an. Joseph's dream is mentioned in 12:4, while his parents' and brothers' prostration to him is reported in 12:100.

Shaytan was looking, also. "Oh! What is this?" objecting. And the first rebel against his Lord, the first troublemaker in creation, was Shaytan because he was looking and saying, "Oh! This is just a person created from clay. But I am created from fire, flames of fire!

"Look—flames of fire! How can it be? How it can be for me to prostrate to a creation that is just created from clay?" That was his mentality, *"Eşek mantığı,* donkey's mentality," we say. He was saying, "I must be the one who is prostrated to. I am above his creation." He was looking at the material being of Adam, and at himself, also, not seeing in what glory Adam had been dressed and the divine crown put on his head. And then he was thrown out.

Therefore, the *sultan* is that one who is crowned and given glory, and *sultans* are only a few, selected ones. Like prophets, they were elected and selected and chosen. Prophets were chosen ones, but yet people were objecting and saying, "Why? This person is like us, going, coming, eating, drinking, marrying. What is the difference between us? Why is he going to be prostrated to and obeyed—for what?" not looking the reason that he was granted that by the Lord of Heavens.

Now people in the twenty-first century, all people, are looking at everyone based on their outward appearance. Shaytan has just made people not to believe in any other aspect, any other title for mankind, and people are saying, "We are all the same."

No! You are all the same in your physical being, but what you represent is not the same. Chosen people, prophets, were dressed in glory from Heavens, but you are not dressed in it. You must look at *his* position that he is coming with, and people have been ordered to be obedient to that one.

Before, up to the end of the nineteenth century, the line of kings and *sultans* was continuing, but Shaytan was working to make a false picture, to make kingdoms seem like something not good, and he was trying to take away that line of kings and to teach people, "All of you, you can dress as kings and *sultans* dressed."

No! They were dressed from Heavens, and even if you could dress in their clothes, you are not like kings or *sultans* who have been dressed in glory from Heavens. That is the main source of the troubles of mankind in the twenty-first century, because everyone is trying to show that they are *something*. "We are kings, we are queens, we are *sultans*."

No. Men can't give honour to a man. It is impossible. Honour, real honour, is a grant from the Lord of Heavens, coming from Heavens, not from people. Don't think that "President" or "Prime Minister" or "Minister" or such titles give a person real honour. No. When you take away their special clothing, they are going to be nothing. When they dress in such clothes, they think they are something. When they are taken from them, they see, "Oh, we are nothing."

People can't give you a title because those who give you a title expect that one day, maybe we will also be given a title by people. "We must try to get more votes. Bring so many peasants—doesn't matter! They do not need to be educated people. This is democracy! No need for clever ones; no-mind people will do, also. Important is to bring thousands and thousands. Even if people don't understand anything, doesn't matter. It is written that, 'Oh-h! One million people voted for that person. This one must be dressed according to his new title.'"

A million people can't give anything to you! A real title is the one that Allah Almighty gives. Shaytan was looking and asking to be honoured or to be granted that honour. And now people are working on that point.

What we are saying is, "O people! The honour of mankind, that is important. And Allah Almighty chose one among mankind to be on behalf of Him, Almighty, to address people through a person. And he, the chosen one, is only one."

Allah Almighty is not calling everyone to be granted a book, as ignorant people were saying, "Why was this holy book just given to him? Why is it not coming to us, also?"[4]

That is their ignorance. Allah called one and clothed him and sent to him, saying, "Tell My commands, My orders, to My servants. If they accept, I will make everything prostrate to them because they represent Me."

Once the Prophet ﷺ was going. He met a *badu*, and he said to him, "O *'abd-ullah*, O servant of my Lord, would you like to believe in Allah and in me, and to be Muslim?"

And he said, "Who are you?"

---

[4] 6:157, 74:52,

"I am the representative of the Lord of Heavens. *Ana Muhammadun.*⁵ Say, '*La ilaha illa-Lah, Muhammdu Rasul-Allah.*'"

"Have you any evidence?" that *badu* asked.

And the Prophet said, "I have. O tree, come to me!" Then that tree walked and came in front of the Prophet and made *sajdah* to him. Then it stood up, and the Prophet said, "Go back to your place," and it went back and stood there.

That *badu* said, "Now I believe that you are the representative of the Lord of Heavens. I am saying, '*La ilaha illa-Lah, Muhammdu Rasul-Allah.*'"

Yes, evidence. There must be evidence. If you have been given an order by Allah Almighty, you must be granted such power. Trees were prostrating; animals were coming and prostrating in front of the Seal of Prophets. Otherwise, no.

Common people are asking to see such evidence. But those who work through their minds, if reciting one verse, *"Alif lam mim,"*⁶ it is enough. No one can say anything like this. You can't find it in any book. *Haybat*, the greatness of the Lord's heavenly Book, heavenly address, in saying *"Alif lam mim,"* makes a man come and prostrate to the one who brought that holy book, holy address. If the Prophet had not been like that, how, for fifteen centuries, would Islam have stood up, in spite of all the shaytans, all

---

⁵"I am Muhammad."

⁶These Arabic letters occur at the beginning of the second *surah* of the Qur'an, and other such letters occur at the beginning of several other *surahs*. Their meaning is known to Allah Almighty, His Prophet, and the select among the holy people of Islam.

the devils, who wanted to take it away? *They* are going to be taken away, but Islam will stand from earth to Heavens.

May Allah forgive me and bless you! For the honour of the most honoured one, Sayyidina Muhammad ﷺ— *Fateha!* ▲

Glossary

Abu Bakr as-Siddiq—the closest of the Prophet's Companions and his father-in-law, who shared the Hijrah with him. After the Prophet's death, he was chosen by consensus of the Muslims as the first caliph or successor to the Prophet. He is known as one of the most saintly of the Prophet's Companions.

'Abdul-Khaliq al-Ghujdawani—the eleventh grandsheikh of the Naqshbandi *tariqah*, one of the Khwajagan of Central Asia.

Abu Hanifa—founder of one of the four schools of Islamic jurisprudence, the Hanafi *madhhab*.

Abu Yazid Bistami—Bayazid Bistami, a great ninth century *wali* and Naqshbandi master.

Adab—good manners, proper etiquette.

Adhan—the call to prayer.

Ahl al-Bayt—People of the House, that is, the family of the Holy Prophet ﷺ.

Ahl ad-dunya—people of the world, i.e., those who are attached to its life and pleasures.

Akhirah—the Hereafter, the Eternal Life.

Alhamdulillah—praise be to Allah, praise God.

Allahu akbar—God is the Most Great.

Amir (pl., 'umara)—chief, leader, head of a nation or people.

Anbiya (plural of **nabi**)—prophets.

'Aql—mind, intellect, intelligence, reason, discernment.

'Arafat—a vast plain outside Mecca where pilgrims gather for the principal rite of Hajj.

'Arif—knower; in the present context, one who has reached spiritual knowledge of his Lord.

Ar-Raheem—the Mercy-Giving, Merciful, Munificent, one of Allah's ninety-nine Holy Names

Ar-Rahman—the Most Merciful, Compassionate, Beneficent, the most often repeated of Allah's Holy Names.

Ashhadu an la ilaha illa-Llah wa ashhadu anna Muhammadu Rasul-Allah—"I bear witness that there is no deity except Allah and I bear witness that Muhammad is Allah's messenger," the Islamic *Shahadah* or Declaration of Faith.

Astaghfirullah—I seek Allah's forgiveness.

A'udhu bil-Lahi min ash-Shaytani-r-Rajeem—I seek refuge in God from Satan the accursed.

Awliya (sing., wali)—the "friends" of Allah, Muslim saints or holy people.

Bayt al-Maqdis— the Sacred House in Jerusalem, built at the site where Solomon's Temple was later erected.

Barakah—blessings.

Batil—vain or false; falsehood, deception.

Bayah—pledge; in the context of this book, the pledge of a disciple (murid) to a sheikh.

Bi-hurmati-l-Fatehah—for the honor or respect of Surat al-Fatehah (the opening chapter of the Qur'an).

Bismillahi-r-Rahmani-r-Raheem—"In the name of Allah, the Beneficent, the Merciful," the invocation with which all a Muslim's actions are supposed to begin.

Dajjal—the False Messiah whom the Prophet ﷺ foretold as coming at the end-time of this world, who will deceive mankind with pretensions of being divine.

Day of Promises—the occasion in the spiritual world when Allah Almighty called together the souls of all human beings to come and asked them to acknowledge His Lordship and sovereignty (7:172).

Dhikr (zikr, zikir)—message, remembrance or reminder, used

in the Qur'an to refer to the Qur'an and other revealed scriptures. Dhikr (or dhikr-Allah) also refers to remembering Allah through repetition of His Holy Names or various phrases of glorification (for the meanings of the phrases of dhikr mentioned in this book, see the footnote entries under individual phrases).

Du'a—supplication, personal prayer.

Dunya—this world and its attractions, worldly involvements.

Efendi—mister, sir.

'Eid—festival; the two major festivals of Islam are 'Eid al-Fitr, marking the completion of Ramadan, and 'Eid al-Adha, the Festival of Sacrifice during the time of Hajj.

Fard—obligatory, prescribed.

Fard al-kifayah – an obligation which suffices to be met by one or a few persons in a community.

Fatehah—al-Fatehah, the opening surah or chapter of the Qur'an.

Fitnah (pl., **fitan**)—trial, test, temptation; also, discord, dissension.

Grandshaykh—a wali of great stature. In this text, where spelled with a capital "G," "Grandshaykh" refers to Mawlana 'Abdullah ad-Daghestani, Shaykh Nazim's shaykh, to whom he was closely attached for forty years up to the time of Grandshaykh's death in 1973.

Hadith (pl., **ahadith**)—a report of the Holy Prophet's sayings, contained in the collections of early hadith scholars. In this text, "Hadith" has been used to refer to the entire body of his oral traditions, while "hadith" denotes an individual tradition.

Halal—lawful, permissible.

Hajji—one who has performed Hajj, the sacred pilgrimage of Islam.

Halal—permitted, lawful according to the Islamic Shari'ah.

Haqq—truth, reality.

Haram—forbidden, unlawful.

Hasha—God forbid! Never!

Haqq—truth, reality.

Haram—prohibited, unlawful.

Hasan al-Basri – a great scholar of the seventh century C.E.

Hawa—desires, lusts, passions of the lower self or nafs.

Hidayah/hidayat—guidance.

Hijab—barrier, screen, veil or curtain; the covering of Muslim women.

Himmah—desire, zeal, eagerness, ambition, determination.

Hu—the divine pronoun, He.

Ibrahim–the prophet Abraham.

Imam—leader; specifically, the leader of a congregational prayer.

Iman—faith, belief.

Iman—faith, belief.

Insha'Allah – God willing, if God wills.

'Isa—the prophet Jesus ﷺ.

'Isha – night; specifically, the night prayer.

Jababirah—tyrants, oppressors.

Jinn—an invisible order of beings created by Allah from fire.

Kafir—a denier or rejector; in an Islamic context, one who denies Allah (an unbeliever or atheist) or does not acknowledge or is ungrateful for divine favors.

Khalifah—deputy, successor, vice-gerent.

Khidr—a holy man, mentioned in the Qur'an, 18:60-82, to whom God has granted life up to the end of the world..

Kufr—unbelief, denial of Allah.

La hawla wa la quwwata illa bil-Lah al-'Aliyi-l-'Azheem— "There is no might nor power except in Allah, the Most High, the All-Mighty," words that Muslims utter frequently during their daily lives , signifying total reliance upon Allah.

La ilaha illa-Llah, Muhammadu rasul-Allah—there is no deity except Allah, Muhammad is the Messenger of Allah.

Mahdi–the divinely-appointed guide whose coming at the end-time of this world is mentioned in several authoritative hadiths. He will lead the believers and establish a rule of justice and righteousness for a period of time prior to the events preceding the end of the world and the Last Judgment.

Masha'Allah—what or as Allah willed.

Masjid—literally, a place where sujud, prostration, is made, i.e., a mosque.

Mawla—master, lord, protector, patron, referring to Allah Most High.

Me'raj—the Holy Prophet's ascension to the Heavens and the Divine Presence.

Muezzin—one who makes the call to prayer (adhan).

Muluk (sing., **malik**)—kings, monarchs.

Mumin/muminah—male/female believers in Islam.

Munkar—that which is disapproved, rejected or considered abominable in Islam.

Murid—a disciple or follower of a shaykh.

Murshid—spiritual guide, pir.

Musa—the prophet Moses ﷺ.

Muwahhid—one who proclaims the Unity of Allah Almighty.

Nafs—(1) soul, self, person; (2) the lower self, the ego.

Nasihah—good advice or counsel, admonition, reminder.

Nur—light.

Qada wa qadar—the sixth pillar of Islamic faith, referring to the divine decree.

Qiblah—direction; specifically, the direction of Mecca.

Qisas—retaliation.

Qiyamat/Qiyamah—the Day of Resurrection.

Rabi'ah al-'Adawiyah—Rabi'ah Basri, a great womansaint of the eighth century C.E.

Rabitah—bond, connection, tie, link, in the context of this book, with a shaykh.

Rak'at—a cycle or unit of the Islamic prayer (salat), which is repeated a specified number of times in each prayer.

Ramadan—the ninth month of the Islamic lunar calendar, the month of fasting.

Rasul-Allah—the Messenger of God, Muhammad ﷺ.

Sahabah (sing., sahabi)—the Companions of the Prophet, the first Muslims.

Sajdah (also sujud)—prostration.

Salat—the prescribed Islamic prayer or worship.

Sallallahu 'alayhi was-sallam—Islamic invocation on the Prophet ﷺ, meaning, "May Allah's peace and blessings be upon him."

Salawat—invoking blessings and peace upon the Holy Prophet ﷺ.

Sayyid—leader; also, a descendant of the Holy Prophet.

Sayyidina—our chief, master.

Sayyidina 'Ali—the cousin and son-in-law of the Prophet ﷺ and the fourth caliph of Islam.

Sayyidina 'Umar—'Umar ibn al-Khattab, the Prophet's eminent Companion and the second caliph of Islam.

Shahadah—the Islamic creed or Declaration of Faith, "Ash-shadu an la ilaha illa-Llah wa ashhadu anna Muhammu rasul Allah, I bear witness that there is no deity except Allah and I bear witness that Muhammad is His messenger."

Shah Naqshband—Grandshaykh Muhammad Bahauddin Shah-Naqshband, a great eighth century wali, the founder of the Naqshbandi Tariqah.

Shari'at/Shari'ah—the divine Law of Islam, based on the Qur'an and the Sunnah of the Prophet ﷺ.

Shirk—polytheism/idolatry, ascribing divinity or divine attributes to anything other than God.

Shaykh Sharafuddin—the shaykh of Grandshaykh 'Abdullah ad-Daghistani.

Shaytan—Satan.

Sohbet (Arabic, **suhbah**)—a shaykh's discourse (association).

Subhanallah—glory be to Allah.

Sultan al-Awliya—lit., "the king of the awliya,' the highest ranking saint.

Sunnah—the practice of the Holy Prophet; that is, what he did, said, recommended or approved of in his Companions. In this text, "Sunnah" is used to refer to the collective body of his actions, sayings or recommendations, while "sunnah" refers to an individual action or recommendation.

Surah—chapter of the Qur'an.

Takbeer—the pronouncement of God's greatness, "Allahu akbar, God is Most Great."

Taraweeh—the special nighly prayers of Ramadan.

Tariqah/tariqat—literally, way, road or path. An Islamic order or path of discipline and devotion under the guidance of a shaykh (*pir, wali*); Islamic Sufism.

Tawaf—the rite of circumambulatin the K'abah while glorifying Allah, one of the rites of Hajj and 'Umrah.

'Ulama (sing, **'alim**)—scholars, specifically of Islam.

'Umar—see Sayyidina **'Umar**.

Ummah—faith community, nation.

'Umrah—the minor pilgrimage to Mecca, which can be performed at any time of the year.

Uns – familiarity.

Wali (pl., **awliya**)—a Muslim holy man or saint.

Wa min Allah at-tawfeeq—And success is only from Allah.

Wudu—the prescribed minor ablution preceding prayers and other acts of worship.

Ya Rabb—O Lord.

Zakat/zakah—the obligatgory charity of Islam, one of its five "pillars" or acts of worship.

Zakat al-Fitr—the obligatory charity of 'Eid al-Fitr, the festival marking the completion of Ramadan.

Zhulm (zulm)—injustice, oppression, tyranny, misuse, transgressing proper limits, wrongdoing.

OTHER TITLES FROM
THE INSTITUTE FOR SPIRITUAL & CULTURAL ADVANCEMENT

Online ordering available from www.isn1.net

THE PATH TO SPIRITUAL EXCELLENCE
By Shaykh Muhammad Nazim Adil al-Haqqani
ISBN 1-930409-18-4, Paperback. 180 pp.

This compact volume provides practical steps to purify the heart and overcome the destructive characteristics that deprive us of peace and inner satisfaction. On this amazing journey doubt, fear, and other negative influences that plague our lives - and which we often pass on to our children - can be forever put aside. Simply by introducing in our daily lives those positive thought patterns and actions that attract divine support, we can reach spiritual levels that were previously inaccessible.

IN THE MYSTIC FOOTSTEPS OF SAINTS
By Shaykh Muhammad Nazim Adil al-Haqqani
Volume 1 - ISBN 1-930409-05-2
Volume 2 – ISBN 1-930409-09-5
Volume 3 – ISBN 1-930409-13-3, Paperback. Ave. length 200 pp.

Narrated in a charming, old-world storytelling style, this highly spiritual series offers several volumes of practical guidance on how to establish serenity and peace in daily life, heal emotional and spiritual scars, and discover the role we are each destined to play in the universal scheme.

CLASSICAL ISLAM & THE NAQSHBANDI SUFI TRADITION
By Shaykh Muhammad Hisham Kabbani
ISBN 1-930409-23-0, Hardback. 950 pp.
ISBN 1-930409-10-9, Paperback. 744 pp.

This esteemed work includes an unprecedented historical narrative of the forty saints of the renowned Naqshbandi Golden Chain, dating back to Prophet Muhammad in the early seventh century. With close personal ties to the most recent saints, the author has painstakingly compiled rare accounts of their miracles, disciplines, and how they have lent spiritual support throughout the world for fifteen centuries. Traditional Islam and the Naqshbandi Sufi Tradition is a shining tribute to developing human relations at the highest level, and the power of spirituality to uplift humanity from its lower nature to that of spiritual triumph.

GUIDEBOOK OF DAILY PRACTICES AND DEVOTIONS
By Shaykh Muhammad Hisham Kabbani
ISBN 1-930409-22-2, Paperback. 352 pp.

This book details the spiritual practices which have enabled devout seekers to awaken certainty of belief and to attain stations of nearness to the Divine Presence. This detailed compilation, in English, Arabic and transliteration, includes the daily personal dhikr as well as the rites performed with every obligatory prayer, rites for holy days and details of the pilgrimage to Mecca and the visit of Prophet Muhammad in Madinah.

Naqshbandi *Awrad* of Shaykh Nazim
Compiled by Shaykh Muhammad Hisham Kabbani
ISBN 1-930409-06-0, Paperback. 104 pp.

This book presents in detail, in both English, Arabic and transliteration, the daily, weekly and date-specific devotional rites of Naqshbandi practitioners, as prescribed by the world guide of the Naqshbandi-Haqqani Sufi Order, Mawlana Shaykh Muhammad Nazim Adil al-Haqqani.

Pearls and Coral, I & II
By Shaykh Muhammad Hisham Kabbani
ISBN 1-930409-07-9, Paperback. 220 pp.
ISBN 1-930409-08-7, Paperback. 220 pp.

A series of lectures on the unique teachings of the Naqshbandi Order, originating in the Near East and Central Asia, which has been highly influential in determining the course of human history in these regions. Always pushing aspirants on the path of Gnosis to seek higher stations of nearness to the God, the Naqshbandi Masters of Wisdom melded practical methods with deep spiritual wisdom to build an unequalled methodology of ascension to the Divine Presence.

The Sufi Science of Self-Realization
By Shaykh Muhammad Hisham Kabbani
ISBN 1-930409-29-X, Paperback. 244 pp.

The path from submersion in the negative traits to the unveiling of these six powers is known as migration to Perfected Character. Through a ten-step program, the author--a master of the Naqshbandi Sufi Path--describes the science of eliminating the seventeen ruinous characteristics of the tyrannical ego, to achieve purification of the soul. The sincere seeker who follows these steps, with devotion and discipline, will acheive an unveiling of the six powers which lie dormant within every human heart.

ENCYCLOPEDIA OF ISLAMIC DOCTRINE
Shaykh Muhammad Hisham Kabbani
ISBN: 1-871031-86-9, Paperback, Vol. 1-7.

The most comprehensive treatise on Islamic belief in the English language. The only work of its kind in English, Shaykh Hisham Kabbani's seven volume Encyclopedia of Islamic Doctrine is a monumental work covering in great detail the subtle points of Islamic belief and practice. Based on the four canonical schools of thought, this is an excellent and vital resource to anyone seriously interested in spirituality. There is no doubt that in retrospect, this will be the most significant work of this age.

THE APPROACH OF ARMAGEDDON?
by Shaykh Muhammad Hisham Kabbani
ISBN 1-930409-20-6, Paperback 292 pp.

This unprecedented work is a "must read" for those interested in broadening their understanding of centuries-old religious traditions pertaining to the Last Days. This book chronicles scientific breakthroughs and world events of the Last Days as foretold by Prophet Muhammad. Also included are often concealed ancient predictions of Islam regarding the appearance of the anti-Christ, Armageddon, the leadership of believers by Mahdi ("the Savior"), the second coming of Jesus Christ, and the tribulations preceding the Day of Judgment. We are given final hope of a time on earth filled with peace, reconciliation, and prosperity; an age in which enmity and wars will end, while wealth is overflowing. No person shall be in need and the entire focus of life will be spirituality."

KEYS TO THE DIVINE KINGDOM
By Shaykh Muhammad Hisham Kabbani
ISBN 1-930409-28-1, Paperback. 140 pp.

God said, "We have created everything in pairs." This has to do with reality versus imitation. Our physical form here in this earthly life is only a reflection of our heavenly form. Like plastic fruit and real fruit, one is real, while the other is an imitation. This book looks at the nature of the physical world, the laws governing the universe and from this starting point, jumps into the realm of spiritual knowledge - Sufi teachings which must be "tasted" as opposed to read or spoken. It will serve to open up to the reader the mystical path of saints which takes human beings from the world of forms and senses to the world within the heart, the world of gnosis and spirituality - a world filled with wonders and blessings.

MY LITTLE LORE OF LIGHT
By Hajjah Amina Adil
ISBN 1-930409-35-4, Paperback, 204 pp.

A children's version of Hajjah Amina Adil's four volume work, *Lore Of Light*, this books relates the stories of God's prophets, from Adam to Muhammad, upon whom be peace, drawn from traditional Ottoman sources. This book is intended to be read aloud to young children and to be read by older children for themselves. The stories are shortened and simplified but not changed. The intention is to introduce young children to their prophets and to encourage thought and discussion in the family about the eternal wisdom these stories embody.

MUHAMMAD: THE MESSENGER OF ISLAM
By Hajjah Amina Adil
ISBN 1-930409-11-7, Paperback. 608 pp.

Since the 7th century, the sacred biography of Islam's Prophet Muhammad has shaped the perception of the religion and its place in world history. This book skilfully etches the personal portrait of a man of incomparable moral and spiritual stature, as seen through the eyes of Muslims around the world. Compiled from classical Ottoman Turkish sources and translated into English, this comprehensive biography is deeply rooted in the life example of its prophet.

CPSIA information can be obtained at www.ICGtesting.com
Printed in the USA
LVOW05s1833040514

384380LV00001B/375/P